QuickBooks Online Practice Set

Gain Experience with Realistic Transactions

Michelle L. Long, CPA, MBA

Andrew S. Long, CPA

DEDICATION

This book is dedicated to all the accountants, bookkeepers and QuickBooks Online users who want more practice using QuickBooks Online. We created this practice set for you to gain more experience and confidence using QuickBooks Online.

MICHELLE L. LONG AND ANDREW S. LONG

ABOUT THE AUTHORS

Michelle L. Long, CPA, MBA is the founder of Long for Success, LLC specializing in QuickBooks training, consulting and app integrations. She consults with Intuit and other companies who are developing products and/or services for the industry (QuickBooks related) and provides other advisory services for accounting professionals and small business owners.

Michelle is an internationally recognized trainer and expert and has taught QuickBooks since 1999. Since 2007, she's been a contract trainer for Intuit and taught QuickBooks in cities across the U.S., Canada, Australia and in London. Plus, she's taught numerous webinars for Intuit, Staples, Office Depot, QB Power Hour and more. She's authored and co-authored numerous courses for Intuit including the Advanced Certification exams (desktop and Online) and other topics including marketing and pricing strategies.

Michelle is the author of the books Successful QuickBooks Online Consulting: The Comprehensive Guide to Starting and Growing a QuickBooks Online Consulting Business, How to Start a Home-Based Bookkeeping Business, and co-author of QuickBooks On Demand and the QuickBooks Practice Sets (all books are available on Amazon).

Michelle is a CPA, Advanced Certified QuickBooks Online ProAdvisor, holds an MBA in Entrepreneurship and is a Certified FastTrac Facilitator. She has received numerous awards and recognitions including: Most Powerful Women in Accounting (by CPA Practice Advisor), 10 Women who Inspire a Profession (by Accounting Today), a Top 10 ProAdvisor (3 times by Insightful Accountant), a Top 100 Small Business Influencer by Small Business Trends, and a Financial Services Champion of the Year by the Small Business Administration in recognition of her dedication to helping entrepreneurs and small business owners.

Andrew S. Long, CPA graduated with a MS in Accountancy from the University of Missouri – Columbia in December 2013. Andrew made the Dean's List every semester and he earned numerous scholarships for his academic achievements. Andrew was selected as a member of the prestigious Cornell Leadership Program. He was a member of the Flegel Academy of Aspiring Entrepreneurs and a member of Beta Alpha Psi.

Andrew has worked as a staff accountant and senior accountant for a real estate company in Columbia, Missouri. He likes water and snow skiing and enjoying the outdoors.

Contents

ACKNOWLEDGEMENTS

Special thanks to the following individuals for help in reviewing the QuickBooks Practice set which was modified for this QuickBooks Online Practice Set:

Jack E. Cole, Jr.
C*C Systems & Software

Jim Knapp
Knapp Consulting

Janice Boggs
JB's Accounting Solutions

Jo Ellen Peters
Top Notch Bookkeeping

Paula Small
Small Stepping Stones

Author: Please direct your comments or suggestions for future editions to michelle@longforsuccess.com or www.LongforSuccess.com.

1 INTRODUCTION

This practice set is designed to provide realistic transactions for a fictional business (Fitness Haven, LLC) to provide experience using QuickBooks Online. You will set up a new company file, enter three months of transactions, reconcile accounts and check your progress at the end of each month.

This practice set is designed to be used with QuickBooks Online Plus. Go to http://www.QuickBooksOnline.com to register for a free 30 day trial. Instead of using your regular email address (use it for your regular QuickBooks Online file), use an alternative email for the free trial to use for this practice set.

QuickBooks Online is updated frequently so you may notice some differences in the images. However, you should still be able to enter transactions, reconcile and create reports for this practice set.

This practice set does **not** teach you QuickBooks Online nor accounting or bookkeeping principles. It provides an opportunity for you to get more experience using QuickBooks Online. The ability to check your progress with various reports helps verify that you are entering transactions correctly.

Additionally, this practice set does **not** address nor discuss accounting principles that may vary according to the type of business entity, industry, etc. To simplify this practice set, Fitness Haven, LLC (the fictitious company used in the practice set) does **not** follow GAAP -- i.e. this exercise does not address unearned revenues on membership dues, depreciation on fixed assets, etc. The focus of this practice set is entering transactions common to most small businesses in QuickBooks Online, reconciling and generating reports.

There is a sample company you can use for more practice on your own. You can access it at http://qbo.intuit.com/redir/testdrive

Fitness Haven

In this practice set, business partners Tom Martin, Joe Watson, and Nancy Clemens decide to open a neighborhood fitness center called Fitness Haven. They have been discussing the idea for years and finally decided to take the leap and start the business.

The partners will combine money from their savings and take out a bank loan to finance the gym. They have agreed to forgo a salary or compensation for themselves and to not hire any employees until the business is financially stable (i.e. in the practice set there is no payroll, owner's draws or guaranteed payments).

They will manually write checks and use a credit card for purchases. They plan on buying all the equipment and supplies and leasing (renting) the space for Fitness Haven at a popular neighborhood shopping center. The space they are leasing will need remodeling (leasehold improvements) to get it ready to open. They will purchase exercise equipment and offer classes and personal training sessions in addition to monthly or quarterly memberships.

There will be some retail sales from a few inventory items (bottled water, sports drinks, and nutrition bars). They will purchase a cash register and record weekly sales summaries of these retail sales in QuickBooks Online. All sales are cash or check only (i.e. they do not accept credit cards payments from customers).

You will start by setting up a new company file for Fitness Haven in QuickBooks Online. Next, you will enter transactions during the start-up phase for the first month (January). Then, there are transactions for the next two months (February and March) as well. There are several reports at the end of each month for you to check your work and make corrections if needed.

NOTE: Your QuickBooks Online reports will probably look different from the ones in this practice set. To fit the pertinent information from the report onto the page, we customized many reports (i.e. removed columns, changed the width of columns or made other formatting changes). Focus on the content of the reports (the numbers and details) to check your progress.

If you want to start over or go through the practice set again, you will need to set up another trial subscription to QuickBooks Online (using a different email address).

Note: Please pay attention to the notes throughout the practice set. They contain helpful information.

2 SET UP A NEW COMPANY

First, enter the company name shown in the box below and select less than 1 year for the how long have you been in business box in QuickBooks Online and then click Next. Do not check the option to import data from QuickBooks Desktop. Check the first six boxes for send and track invoices, organize your expenses, manage your inventory, track your retail sales, track your bills, and track your sales tax. Do not select pay your employees or track hours. QBO will now take you to the main screen. From there click the settings wheel in the upper right corner and click on accounts and settings. Click on the pencil icons on the right to input the rest of the information in the boxes below starting with the EIN. Select Partnership for the tax form (Form 1065) and enter Fitness and Recreational Sports Centers for the industry.

Company name (and Legal Name)	Employer ID Number (EIN)	Phone	Address
Fitness Haven, LLC	99-7654321	(654) 555-3476	2601 N Meadow Ln Springfield, IA 68432

Next, from the accounts and settings menu click the Sales tab on the left side and make sure track inventory quantity on hand is turned on. Now click the Expenses tab and turn on purchase orders. Click Save and then click Done on the bottom right. Leave the other fields on their default setting.

Note: You may need to disable your browser from blocking pop ups as they are frequently used in QuickBooks Online to set up accounts or items.

MICHELLE L. LONG AND ANDREW S. LONG

Modify the Chart of Accounts

1. Open the Chart of Accounts (select Accounting on the left side and then select chart of accounts) to add new accounts (Partner's Equity) for Tom, Joe, and Nancy so the equity accounts (with sub-accounts for Partner Contributions and Distributions) are as follows:

- Tom Martin
    - Tom Partner Contribution
    - Tom Partner Distributions

- Joe Watson
    - Joe Partner Contribution
    - Joe Partner Distributions

- Nancy Clemens
    - Nancy Partner Contribution
    - Nancy Partner Distributions

Note: To set up Tom's accounts, select New (on the upper right of the chart of accounts page) > Choose Equity under Account Type > Partner's Equity under Detail Type > enter "Tom Martin" in the name field and click Save. Follow the same process to create the two sub-accounts except select "Partner Contributions" and "Partner Distributions" under Detail Type and check the box "is sub-account" and select the parent account "Tom Martin" and then hit Save. Repeat the steps to step up Joe's and Nancy's accounts.

2. Add a Credit Card type account named: Visa

3. Add a Long Term Liability account named: Note Payable – Hometown Bank

4. Add Income accounts (Service/Fee Income type) named Registration Fees and Gym Revenues (for membership fees, classes, and personal training sessions).

Set up Products and Services

First, add a new Sales Tax Item for Springfield payable to Iowa Department of Revenue. Select Taxes > Sales Tax on the main menu bar on the left side, click to set up sales tax, select No on the question for do you need to collect tax outside Iowa. Select Quarterly for the filing frequency and enter January 1st of the current year for the start date and click Next to complete the set up.

Now go to the Products and Services List (Click the settings gear icon on the upper right and select Products and Services under the Lists section) to add Service items for the monthly classes and personal training sessions. Set up the items to post to the Gym Revenues income account. The classes are $50 each and personal training sessions are $35 an hour. Both are non-taxable (uncheck the Is taxable box).

- Personal Training - $35
- Basic Fitness 101 - $50
- Kardio Killers - $50
- Wicked Weights - $50
- Yoga Fitness - $50

Add the following non-taxable service item (uncheck the Is taxable box) to post to the Registration Fees income account:

- Registration Fee ($25)

Add the following non-taxable service items to post to the Gym Revenues income account:

- Monthly Membership ($35)
- Quarterly Membership ($90)

Set up Inventory on Products and Services List

Fitness Haven will have a few food items (drinks and nutrition bars) available for sale. A cash register will be used to record the sale of food items (inventory). A weekly summary of sales will be recorded in QuickBooks Online as a Sales Receipt. All sales are paid with cash or checks (no credit cards are accepted from customers).

Note: Important information about setting up inventory on the products and services list:

- Enter each product as an inventory item, enter initial quantity on hand as 0, and **change as of date to January 1 of the current year.**

- Flavor varieties should be set up as belonging to the category they are under. So the inventory item Lemon will be under the Sports Drink category, Regular is under the Energy Drink category etc. The categories do not need to be set up as unique items but will need to be added in the category box the first time you use each one.

- All products should be posted to Sales of Product Income and Cost of Goods Sold

- Leave the "Is taxable" box under sales information checked and leave all other fields blank.

Note: Keyboard shortcuts help speed it up – tab through the fields (or use Control+tab to go back through fields) and use the space bar to check a box. Alt+S will save. Creating an Excel file to import them may be more efficient than entering each one individually (but not needed for this practice set).

Item	Unit Cost	Sales Price
Bottled Water	$0.17	$1.50
Sports Drink:		
Lemon	0.37	2.00
Orange	0.37	2.00
Blue	0.37	2.00
Red	0.37	2.00
Energy Drink:		
Regular	1.05	3.75
Sugar-Free	1.05	3.75

Nutrition Bar:		
Chocolate	0.45	3.25
Vanilla	0.45	3.25
Peanut Butter	0.45	3.25

Add New Vendors:

Add the vendors in the table below by hovering over the Expenses tab on the left hand menu and then clicking Vendors.

Company	Address	Phone	1099 – ID #
Copper Property Management Co.	423 Eagle Rd Springfield, IA 68432	(654) 555-0122	
Curtis Contractors	8465 Blue Creek Dr Springfield, IA 68432	(654) 555-4876	99-1234567 (Check box to track payments for 1099)
Jones Law Firm	493 Bison Ct Springfield, IA 68432	(654) 555-0937	20-0983456 (Check box to track payments for 1099)
Life Fitness Co.	12576 Trailview Rd Springfield, IA 68432	(654) 555-4069	

Add New Customers:

Add the customers in the table below by hovering over the Sales tab on the left hand menu and then clicking Customers, New Customer.

Customer	Address	Phone
Adrian Gonzalez	324 Birdsong Way Springfield, IA 68432	(654) 555-5632
Daniel Brown	782 Locust Ave Springfield, IA 68432	(654) 555-5890
Lucy Hopper	8326 Waterfall Ln Springfield, IA 68432	(654) 555-6264

Throughout the Practice Set, as you enter transactions for new customers or vendors, use the Quick Add feature to add them. **Note**: this practice set contains address information only. In a real business situation, you may need to include more details such as emails, terms, custom fields or more.

Check your Progress

Chart of Accounts

Here is what the Chart of Accounts looks like. You can access this report by clicking on Reports and type "account list" in the search bar.

Note: Make sure accrual basis is selected for reports whenever the option appears (it won't always and should be in accrual by default).

Note: For this and all other reports shown throughout the practice set, the reports were modified to show only the most relevant information due to space restrictions so your reports may look different. For example, in this report all columns were removed except the three most important columns as shown here. Most of these were first exported to Excel which is handy if you want to manipulate the data.

Account	Type	Detail type
Inventory	Other Current Assets	Inventory
Inventory Asset	Other Current Assets	Inventory
Uncategorized Asset	Other Current Assets	Other Current Assets
Undeposited Funds	Other Current Assets	Undeposited Funds
Visa	Credit Card	Credit Card
Iowa Department of Revenue Payable	Other Current Liabilities	Sales Tax Payable
Out Of Scope Agency Payable	Other Current Liabilities	Sales Tax Payable
Note Payable - Hometown Bank	Long Term Liabilities	Notes Payable
Joe Watson	Equity	Partner's Equity
Joe Watson:Joe Partner Contributions	Equity	Partner Contributions
Joe Watson:Joe Partner Distributions	Equity	Partner Distributions
Nancy Clemens	Equity	Partner's Equity
Nancy Clemens:Nancy Partner Contributions	Equity	Partner Contributions
Nancy Clemens:Nancy Partner Distributions	Equity	Partner Distributions
Opening Balance Equity	Equity	Opening Balance Equity
Owner's Investment	Equity	Owner's Equity
Owner's Pay & Personal Expenses	Equity	Owner's Equity
Retained Earnings	Equity	Retained Earnings
Tom Martin	Equity	Partner's Equity
Tom Martin:Tom Partner Contributions	Equity	Partner Contributions
Tom Martin:Tom Partner Distributions	Equity	Partner Distributions
Billable Expense Income	Income	Sales of Product Income
Gym Revenues	Income	Service/Fee Income
Registration Fees	Income	Service/Fee Income
Sales	Income	Sales of Product Income
Sales of Product Income	Income	Sales of Product Income
Uncategorized Income	Income	Sales of Product Income

Cost of Goods Sold	Cost of Goods Sold	Supplies & Materials - COGS
Shipping	Cost of Goods Sold	Shipping, Freight & Delivery - COS
Advertising & Marketing	Expenses	Advertising/Promotional
Ask My Accountant	Expenses	Utilities
Bank Charges & Fees	Expenses	Bank Charges
Car & Truck	Expenses	Auto
Contractors	Expenses	Payroll Expenses
Insurance	Expenses	Insurance
Interest Paid	Expenses	Interest Paid
Job Supplies	Expenses	Supplies & Materials
Legal & Professional Services	Expenses	Legal & Professional Fees
Meals & Entertainment	Expenses	Entertainment Meals
Office Supplies & Software	Expenses	Office/General Administrative Expenses
Other Business Expenses	Expenses	Office/General Administrative Expenses
Purchases	Expenses	Supplies & Materials
Reimbursable Expenses	Expenses	Supplies & Materials
Rent & Lease	Expenses	Rent or Lease of Buildings
Repairs & Maintenance	Expenses	Repair & Maintenance
Taxes & Licenses	Expenses	Taxes Paid
Travel	Expenses	Travel
Uncategorized Expense	Expenses	Other Miscellaneous Service Cost
Utilities	Expenses	Utilities
Other Miscellaneous Expense	Other Expense	Other Miscellaneous Expense

Items list

You can access this report by typing "Product/Service List" into the search bar after you click the reports button from the main menu.

Again – only relevant columns are shown here.

Product/Service	Type	Price	Cost	Qty On Hand
Basic Fitness 101	Service	50.00		
Bottled Water	Inventory	1.50	0.17	
Energy Drink:Regular	Inventory	3.75	1.05	
Energy Drink:Sugar-Free	Inventory	3.75	1.05	
Hours	Service			
Kardio Killers	Service	50.00		
Monthly Membership	Service	35.00		
Nutrition Bar:Chocolate	Inventory	3.25	0.45	
Nutrition Bar:Peanut Butter	Inventory	3.25	0.45	
Nutrition Bar:Vanilla	Inventory	3.25	0.45	
Personal Training	Service	35.00		
Quarterly Membership	Service	90.00		
Registration Fee	Service	25.00		
Sales	Service			
Sports Drink:Blue	Inventory	2.00	0.37	
Sports Drink:Lemon	Inventory	2.00	0.37	
Sports Drink:Orange	Inventory	2.00	0.37	
Sports Drink:Red	Inventory	2.00	0.37	
Sports Drink:Sugar-Free	Inventory	3.75	1.05	
Wicked Weights	Service	50.00		
Yoga Fitness	Service	50.00		

Vendors List

You can view the vendors list by typing "Vendor Contact List" into the reports search bar.

Vendor	Phone Numbers	Address
Copper Property Management Co.	Phone: (654) 555-0122	423 Eagle Rd Springfield IA 68432
Curtis Contractors	Phone: (654) 555-4876	8465 Blue Creek Dr Springfield IA 68432
Jones Law Firm	Phone: (654) 555-0937	493 Bison Ct Springfield IA 68432
Life Fitness Co.	Phone: (654) 555-4069	12576 Trailview Rd Springfield IA 68432

Customers List

You can view the customers list by clicking on Reports > Report List > Customer Contact List.

Customer	Phone Numbers	Billing Address	Shipping Address
Adrian Gonzalez	Phone: (654) 555-5632	324 Birdsong Way Springfield IA 68432	324 Birdsong Way Springfield IA 68432
Daniel Brown	Phone: (654) 555-5890	782 Locust Ave Springfield IA 68432	782 Locust Ave Springfield IA 68432
Lucy Hopper	Phone: (654) 555-6264	8326 Waterfall Ln Springfield IA 68432	8326 Waterfall Ln Springfield IA 68432

3 ENTERING TRANSACTIONS – JANUARY

Enter the following transactions for January. For this practice set, post the following transactions to the appropriate account based on the expenditure (i.e. do not post anything to start-up expenses). In a real situation, you should consult with an accountant or tax professional for guidance on accounting for start-up costs.

Notes for entering transactions:

- Use Accounts Payable for monthly expenses and bills. When transactions say "Received a Bill" (you will enter the bill and pay bills when indicated).

- Enter Checks or Credit Card Charges as indicated for purchases from local retailers and others.

- Quick Add Customers and Vendors as needed (the partners should be set up as a vendor).

- Create new accounts as needed and do not worry about depreciation on fixed asset accounts.

Navigating Tips

Google Chrome is the recommended browser for QuickBooks Online and you can download it free (like Firefox or Internet Explorer). In all browsers, you can have multiple tabs or windows open (tabbed browsing). In Chrome, you can right click on the tab and select Duplicate. In other browsers, Control+N (Cmd+N on a Mac) will open another window / browser tab. Plus, you can drag & drop to re-arrange the open tabs or move a window to another monitor. This allows you to have multiple windows open when working in QuickBooks Online which can help improve efficiency. Use Google or Help for your browser to learn more about tabbed browsing.

Additionally, with Google Chrome you can create multiple user accounts. This allows you to login to multiple QuickBooks Online companies simultaneously. However, pay careful attention to the user icon to monitor which company you are currently using. It is easy to make changes to the wrong company file. This article explains how to set up and use multiple users in Google Chrome: https://support.google.com/chrome/answer/2364824?hl=en

January Transactions

1. Jan 4: The partners (Tom Martin, Joe Watson, and Nancy Clemens) contribute $5,000.00 each to open the Fitness Haven checking account at Hometown Bank with an initial deposit totaling $15,000.00.

   Note: Add a bank account (checking) for Hometown Bank (no opening balance). Click on the + button on the top right portion of the screen and select Bank Deposit under the Other section. Type Fitness Haven Checking and when it takes you to the Quick Add screen make sure the account type is Bank and select Checking for the detail type. Enter a deposit for the $15,000 posting it to the Owner's Contribution accounts for each partner. Quick Add each partner as a Vendor so details of their activity will be shown in the Vendor Center.

   TIP: It saves time to set up Online Banking in QuickBooks Online and download transactions. You can practice with downloaded transactions in the sample company here: http://qbo.intuit.com/redir/testdrive -- go to Banking, Downloaded Transactions (or Online Banking).

   TIP: You can use the + or − key to move the date forward or backward quickly as you enter transactions. Also, if you enter T in the date field, it will use Today's date.

2. Jan 7: Deposited loan proceeds of $250,000.00 for the Note Payable from Hometown Bank into checking account.

3. Jan 8: Check #1001 to Copper Property Management Co. in the amount of $4,500.00 ($3,000.00 for security deposit and $1,500.00 for January rent). (Click the Create icon (looks like a plus sign) and select Check under the Vendors section).

   Note: Type Security Deposit and it will prompt you to add the new account, select Other Assets for the account type and Security Deposits under detail type.

4. Jan 9: Check #1002 to Jones Law Firm in the amount of $1,785.00 for legal fees for the partnership agreement.

5. Jan 17: Check #1003 to Curtis Contractors in the amount of $52,736.89 for Leasehold Improvements.

   Note: Create a new fixed asset account for the Leasehold Improvements (found under the Fixed Assets category) and do not check the box to track depreciation or enter an original cost.

6. Jan 18: Check #1004 to Life Fitness Co. in the amount of $80,000.00 for the purchase of exercise equipment.

Fixed Asset Item	Total Price
Treadmills (5)	$10,000
Stationary Bikes (5)	12,000
Elliptical Machines (5)	10,000

Weight Machines (10)	40,000
Free Weights (2 sets)	8,000

Note: QuickBooks Online does not have a fixed asset items list so instead set up a new account called Fitness Equipment as a Machinery & Equipment fixed asset account (choose to not track depreciation and do not enter a cost). Add fixed asset accounts for each of the 5 different kinds of equipment purchased as sub-accounts of the Fitness Equipment account. Put the quantity in the description field of the itemize by account section when writing the check (not when setting up the account).

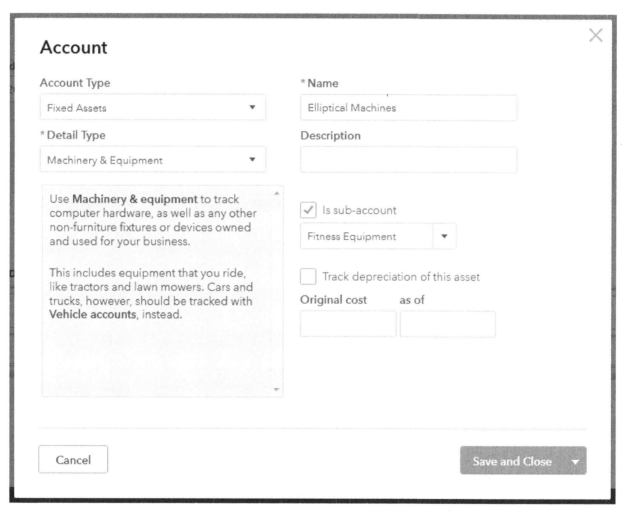

7. Jan 21: Charged $136.67 on Visa credit card at Wal-Mart for office supplies. (Click the + button and click expense under the vendor section). Quick Add Wal-Mart as a vendor and make sure to change the bank/credit account to Visa and payment type to credit card.

8. Jan 21: Check #1005 to Costco in the amount of $2,400 for the following office equipment:

Note: Set up a new account called Office Furniture and Equipment as a Machinery & Equipment fixed asset account (choose to not track depreciation and do not enter a cost). This time you do not need to create a separate account for each item, just note in the description the items purchased.

Fixed Asset Item	Total Price
Cash Register	$1,200
Computer	1,000
Printer	200

9. Jan 22: Purchase order #1001 to Fit Foods, Inc. in the amount of $126.48 to purchase the following inventory items: (Hit the + button, then purchase order, just save it, no need to email it for this exercise)

Item	Quantity	Unit Cost	Total Cost	Sales Price
Bottled Water	48	$0.17	$8.16	$1.50
Sports Drink:				
Lemon	24	0.37	8.88	2.00
Orange	24	0.37	8.88	2.00
Blue	24	0.37	8.88	2.00
Red	24	0.37	8.88	2.00
Energy Drink:				
Regular	24	1.05	25.20	3.75
Sugar-Free	24	1.05	25.20	3.75
Nutrition Bar:				
Chocolate	24	0.45	10.80	3.25
Vanilla	24	0.45	10.80	3.25
Peanut Butter	24	0.45	10.80	3.25

10. Jan 23: Check #1006 to Geek Squad in the amount of $250.00 to set up and configure computers and network (set up an account called Computer and Internet Expense under the Office/General and Administrative Expenses detail type).

11. Jan 25: Check #1007 to Super Signs in the amount of $1,200.00 for purchase of outdoor signage (set up a fixed asset, furniture and fixtures account).

12. Jan 26: Check #1008 to ABC Web Designs in the amount of $300.00 for website creation (a computer and internet expense).

13. Jan 28: Check #1009 to Val-Pak in the amount of $225.00 for advertising in their direct mail packet.

14. Jan 29: Charged $1,723.15 on Visa credit card at Office Depot for the following office furniture:

Fixed Asset Item	Total Price
Desk (2)	$1,567.39
Chairs (2)	155.76

Note: Post it to the Office Furniture and Equipment account and note the items in the description.

15. Jan 31: Received bill from Time Warner in the amount of $147.62 for phone and internet service with terms of net 30 (n/30). (To enter a bill, hit the Create icon at the top of the screen and select bill under the Vendor section).

Note: Make Phone/Internet a sub-account of utilities expense. Also create a sub-account for the each of the following three bills (electricity, water, trash removal).

16. Jan 31: Received bill from Metro Electric Co. in the amount of $183.86 for electricity with terms of n/30.

17. Jan 31: Received bill from City of Springfield in the amount of for $51.45 for water with terms of n/30.

18. Jan 31: Received bill from Waste Management in the amount of $45.00 for trash removal with terms of n/30.

Reconcile Accounts

Use the following information to reconcile the checking account:

Note: To reconcile click the settings wheel on the upper right, select Reconcile under the Tools section, make sure the Checking account is selected and click Reconcile Now. You will need to hit maybe later as QuickBooks will try to connect to an actual bank first but will let you manually reconcile after you decline that option.

Bank Statement Ending Date	1/31/2019 (use current year)
Bank Statement Ending Balance	$122,128.11
Outstanding Checks: Check #1008 -- $300 Check #1009 -- $225	

Use the following information to reconcile the Visa credit card account:

Statement Ending Date	1/31/2019
Statement Ending Balance	$1,859.82
Outstanding Items: None	

Note: You will need to select Visa as the account to be reconciled.

After reconciling the credit card account, select to write a check for payment now before clicking Done. Enter the payment date of Feb. 1, payable to Great American Bank (Quick Add as a vendor). The check number is 1010. If you hit done before doing this, simply write a new check 1010 to Great Bank American Bank with Visa as the account for $1,859.82.

Check Your Progress

Create the following reports and compare them to the results shown (focus on totals – it is ok if accounts are in a different order than what is shown here). Make sure you change the report date for this and all other reports so that it displays the proper period (in this case as of 1/31/19). Throughout this practice set, you may notice the reports shown look different than the reports you generate (some columns missing, different column widths, etc.). This is due space constraints which require customizing the reports to fit in this practice set. These differences are cosmetic only; the numbers shown should match your own.

Note: Select accrual basis for reports when applicable.

Balance Sheet

Note: The easiest way to find each report is to click on the Reports button from the left hand menu and type the name of the report into the search box, in this case Balance Sheet. Click on the report and it will bring it up under the current date, if you entered the dates as shown here, you will need to manually change the dates and click Run Report to rerun the reports with the proper date range.

Fitness Haven, LLC
Balance Sheet
As of January 31, 2019

	Total
ASSETS	
Current Assets	
Bank Accounts	
Fitness Haven Checking	121,603.11
Total Bank Accounts	**$121,603.11**
Other Current Assets	
Inventory Asset	0.00
Total Other Current Assets	**$ 0.00**
Total Current Assets	**$121,603.11**
Fixed Assets	
Fitness Equipment	
Elliptical Machines	10,000.00
Free Weights	8,000.00
Stationary Bikes	12,000.00
Treadmills	10,000.00
Weight Machines	40,000.00
Total Fitness Equipment	**$ 80,000.00**
Leasehold Improvements	52,736.89
Office Furniture and Equipment	4,123.15
Outdoor Signage	1,200.00
Total Fixed Assets	**$138,060.04**
Other Assets	
Security Deposit	3,000.00
Total Other Assets	**$ 3,000.00**
TOTAL ASSETS	**$262,663.15**
LIABILITIES AND EQUITY	
Liabilities	
Current Liabilities	
Accounts Payable	
Accounts Payable (A/P)	427.93

Total Accounts Payable	$	427.93
Credit Cards		
Visa		1,859.82
Total Credit Cards	$	1,859.82
Total Current Liabilities	$	2,287.75
Long-Term Liabilities		
Note Payable - Hometown Bank		250,000.00
Total Long-Term Liabilities		$250,000.00
Total Liabilities		$252,287.75
Equity		
Joe Watson		
Joe Partner Contributions		5,000.00
Total Joe Watson	$	5,000.00
Nancy Clemens		
Nancy Partner Contributions		5,000.00
Total Nancy Clemens	$	5,000.00
Opening Balance Equity		0.00
Retained Earnings		
Tom Martin		
Tom Partner Contributions		5,000.00
Total Tom Martin	$	5,000.00
Net Income		-4,624.60
Total Equity		$ 10,375.40
TOTAL LIABILITIES AND EQUITY		$262,663.15

Profit & Loss

Note: Click the Reports button and start typing Profit and select the Profit & Loss report. The profit and loss and balance sheet are also two of the first three reports displayed at the top of the Reports page.

Fitness Haven, LLC
Profit and Loss
January 2019

	Total
Income	
Total Income	
Gross Profit	$ 0.00
Expenses	
Advertising & Marketing	225.00
Computer and Internet Expense	550.00
Legal & Professional Services	1,785.00
Office Supplies & Software	136.67
Rent & Lease	1,500.00
Utilities	
Electric	183.86
Phone/Internet	147.62
Trash	45.00
Water	51.45
Total Utilities	$ 427.93
Total Expenses	$ 4,624.60
Net Operating Income	-$ 4,624.60
Net Income	-$ 4,624.60

Account Listing

Fitness Haven, LLC
Account List

Account	Type	Detail type	Balance
Fitness Haven Checking	Bank	Checking	119,743.29
Inventory	Other Current Assets	Inventory	0.00
Inventory Asset	Other Current Assets	Inventory	0.00
Uncategorized Asset	Other Current Assets	Other Current Assets	0.00
Undeposited Funds	Other Current Assets	Undeposited Funds	0.00
Fitness Equipment	Fixed Assets	Machinery & Equipment	80,000.00
Fitness Equipment:Elliptical Machines	Fixed Assets	Machinery & Equipment	10,000.00
Fitness Equipment:Free Weights	Fixed Assets	Machinery & Equipment	8,000.00
Fitness Equipment:Stationary Bikes	Fixed Assets	Machinery & Equipment	12,000.00
Fitness Equipment:Treadmills	Fixed Assets	Machinery & Equipment	10,000.00
Fitness Equipment:Weight Machines	Fixed Assets	Machinery & Equipment	40,000.00
Leasehold Improvements	Fixed Assets	Leasehold Improvements	52,736.89
Office Furniture and Equipment	Fixed Assets	Machinery & Equipment	4,123.15
Outdoor Signage	Fixed Assets	Furniture & Fixtures	1,200.00
Security Deposit	Other Assets	Security Deposits	3,000.00
Accounts Payable (A/P)	Accounts payable (A/P)	Accounts Payable (A/P)	-427.93
Visa	Credit Card	Credit Card	0.00
Iowa Department of Revenue Payable	Other Current Liabilities	Sales Tax Payable	0.00
Out Of Scope Agency Payable	Other Current Liabilities	Sales Tax Payable	0.00
Note Payable - Hometown Bank	Long Term Liabilities	Notes Payable	-250,000.00
Joe Watson	Equity	Partner's Equity	-5,000.00
Joe Watson:Joe Partner Contributions	Equity	Partner Contributions	-5,000.00
Joe Watson:Joe Partner Distributions	Equity	Partner Distributions	0.00
Nancy Clemens	Equity	Partner's Equity	-5,000.00
Nancy Clemens:Nancy Partner Contributions	Equity	Partner Contributions	-5,000.00
Nancy Clemens:Nancy Partner Distributions	Equity	Partner Distributions	0.00
Opening Balance Equity	Equity	Opening Balance Equity	0.00
Owner's Investment	Equity	Owner's Equity	0.00
Owner's Pay & Personal Expenses	Equity	Owner's Equity	0.00
Retained Earnings	Equity	Retained Earnings	0.00
Tom Martin	Equity	Partner's Equity	-5,000.00
Tom Martin:Tom Partner Contributions	Equity	Partner Contributions	-5,000.00
Tom Martin:Tom Partner Distributions	Equity	Partner Distributions	0.00
Billable Expense Income	Income	Sales of Product Income	
Gym Revenues	Income	Service/Fee Income	

Registration Fees	Income	Service/Fee Income
Sales	Income	Sales of Product Income
Sales of Product Income	Income	Sales of Product Income
Uncategorized Income	Income	Sales of Product Income
Cost of Goods Sold	Cost of Goods Sold	Supplies & Materials - COGS
Shipping	Cost of Goods Sold	Shipping, Freight & Delivery - COS
Advertising & Marketing	Expenses	Advertising/Promotional
Ask My Accountant	Expenses	Utilities
Bank Charges & Fees	Expenses	Bank Charges
Car & Truck	Expenses	Auto
Computer and Internet Expense	Expenses	Office/General Administrative Expenses
Contractors	Expenses	Payroll Expenses
Insurance	Expenses	Insurance
Interest Paid	Expenses	Interest Paid
Job Supplies	Expenses	Supplies & Materials
Legal & Professional Services	Expenses	Legal & Professional Fees
Meals & Entertainment	Expenses	Entertainment Meals
Office Supplies & Software	Expenses	Office/General Administrative Expenses
Other Business Expenses	Expenses	Office/General Administrative Expenses
Purchases	Expenses	Supplies & Materials
Reimbursable Expenses	Expenses	Supplies & Materials
Rent & Lease	Expenses	Rent or Lease of Buildings
Repairs & Maintenance	Expenses	Repair & Maintenance
Taxes & Licenses	Expenses	Taxes Paid
Travel	Expenses	Travel
Uncategorized Expense	Expenses	Other Miscellaneous Service Cost
Utilities	Expenses	Utilities
Utilities:Electric	Expenses	Utilities
Utilities:Phone/Internet	Expenses	Utilities
Utilities:Trash	Expenses	Utilities
Utilities:Water	Expenses	Utilities
Other Miscellaneous Expense	Other Expense	Other Miscellaneous Expense
Reconciliation Discrepancies	Other Expense	Other Miscellaneous Expense

Accounts Payable Aging Detail

Fitness Haven, LLC
A/P Aging Detail
As of January 31, 2019

	Date	Transaction Type	Num	Vendor	Due Date	Past Due	Amount	Open Balance
Current								
	01/31/2019	Bill		Metro Electric Co.	03/02/2019	-51	183.86	183.86
	01/31/2019	Bill		Time Warner	03/02/2019	-51	147.62	147.62
	01/31/2019	Bill		City of Springfield	03/02/2019	-51	51.45	51.45
	01/31/2019	Bill		Waste Management	03/02/2019	-51	45.00	45.00
Total for Current							$ 427.93	$ 427.93
TOTAL							$ 427.93	$ 427.93

Open Purchase Order List

Fitness Haven, LLC
Open Purchase Order List by Vendor
All Dates

	Date	Num	Memo/Description	Ship Via	Amount	Open Balance
Fit Foods, Inc.						
	01/22/2019	1001			126.48	126.48
Total for Fit Foods, Inc.					$ 126.48	$ 126.48
TOTAL					$ 126.48	$ 126.48

Transaction List by Date

Note: This report can be found under the for my accountant section of the report list.

January 2019

Date	Transaction Type	Num	Posting	Name	Account	Split	Amount
01/01/2019	Inventory Starting Value	START	Yes		Opening Balance Equity	Inventory Asset	0.00
01/01/2019	Inventory Starting Value	START	Yes		Opening Balance Equity	Inventory Asset	0.00
01/01/2019	Inventory Starting Value	START	Yes		Opening Balance Equity	Inventory Asset	0.00
01/01/2019	Inventory Starting Value	START	Yes		Opening Balance Equity	Inventory Asset	0.00
01/01/2019	Inventory Starting Value	START	Yes		Opening Balance Equity	Inventory Asset	0.00
01/01/2019	Inventory Starting Value	START	Yes		Opening Balance Equity	Inventory Asset	0.00
01/01/2019	Inventory Starting Value	START	Yes		Opening Balance Equity	Inventory Asset	0.00
01/01/2019	Inventory Starting Value	START	Yes		Opening Balance Equity	Inventory Asset	0.00
01/01/2019	Inventory Starting Value	START	Yes		Opening Balance Equity	Inventory Asset	0.00
01/01/2019	Inventory Starting Value	START	Yes		Opening Balance Equity	Inventory Asset	0.00
01/01/2019	Inventory Starting Value	START	Yes		Opening Balance Equity	Inventory Asset	0.00
01/01/2019	Inventory Starting Value	START	Yes		Opening Balance Equity	Inventory Asset	0.00
01/04/2019	Deposit		Yes		Fitness Haven Checking	-Split-	15,000.00
01/07/2019	Deposit		Yes		Fitness Haven Checking	Note Payable - Hometown Bank	250,000.00
01/08/2019	Check	1001	Yes	Copper Property Management Co.	Fitness Haven Checking	-Split-	-4,500.00
01/09/2019	Check	1002	Yes	Jones Law Firm	Fitness Haven Checking	Legal & Professional Services	-1,785.00
01/17/2019	Check	1003	Yes	Curtis Contractors	Fitness Haven Checking	Leasehold Improvements	-52,736.89
01/18/2019	Check	1004	Yes	Life Fitness Co.	Fitness Haven Checking	-Split-	-80,000.00
01/21/2019	Expense		Yes	Wal-Mart	Visa	Office Supplies & Software	136.67
01/21/2019	Check	1005	Yes	Costco	Fitness Haven Checking	Office Furniture and Equipment	-2,400.00
01/22/2019	Purchase Order	1001	No	Fit Foods, Inc.	Accounts Payable (A/P)	-Split-	126.48
01/23/2019	Check	1006	Yes	Geek Squad	Fitness Haven Checking	Computer and Internet Expense	-250.00
01/25/2019	Check	1007	Yes	Super Signs	Fitness Haven Checking	Outdoor Signage	-1,200.00
01/26/2019	Check	1008	Yes	ABC Web Designs	Fitness Haven Checking	Computer and Internet Expense	-300.00
01/28/2019	Check	1009	Yes	Val-Pak	Fitness Haven Checking	Advertising & Marketing	-225.00
01/29/2019	Expense		Yes	Office Depot	Visa	Office Furniture and Equipment	1,723.15
01/31/2019	Bill		Yes	Time Warner	Accounts Payable (A/P)	Utilities:Phone/Internet	147.62
01/31/2019	Bill		Yes	Metro Electric Co.	Accounts Payable (A/P)	Utilities:Electric	183.86
01/31/2019	Bill		Yes	City of Springfield	Accounts Payable (A/P)	Utilities:Water	51.45
01/31/2019	Bill		Yes	Waste Management	Accounts Payable (A/P)	Utilities:Trash	45.00

4 ENTERING TRANSACTIONS – FEBRUARY

Fitness Haven opens on February 4th and offers two membership options.

- **Monthly**: New members pay a one-time registration fee of $25 and $35 month membership fees.

- **Quarterly**: Members pay three months of membership dues in advance (only $30 / month). The 3 month membership is non-refundable.

Notes for entering transactions:

- Use a Sales Receipt for initial registration fees and membership dues received. Subsequent membership dues will be entered as an Invoice and then Receive Payment.

- Enter Sales Receipts for classes and personal training sessions.

- Make sure to change Payments received so that they go to Undeposited Funds instead of directly to checking. Leave them in Undeposited Funds until the transaction (weekly) to Record Deposits.

- Use Accounts Payable (i.e. Enter Bills and Pay Bills) for monthly expenses and bills (when transactions say Received Bill and Pay Bills).

- Enter Checks as indicated for purchases from local retailers and others.

- Do not worry about depreciation on fixed assets. It is assumed the accountant or tax professional maintains details of fixed assets and depreciation.

February Transactions

1. Feb 1: Check #1011 to Oak Hill Homeowners Association in the amount of $150.00 for an ad in their newsletter.

2. Feb 3: Check #1012 to Willy's Windows in the amount of $75.00 for window cleaning (repairs and maintenance).

3. Feb 3: Received inventory and the bill ($126.48) from Fit Foods, Inc. for all items ordered on Purchase Order #1, the terms are n/30. (Go to enter a Bill and when you type in Fit Foods as the vendor it will ask if you want to add the purchase order to the bill and click Add).

4. Feb 4: Lucy Steele paid $25 for a first time gym registration fee and a monthly membership fee of $35 (total received $60). (Enter a Sales Receipt, click the Create icon and then click Sales Receipt under the Customers section)

   Note: Use cash or check as the payment method but make sure to change the "Deposit to" box to Undeposited Funds since Fitness Haven only makes weekly deposits. Click Save and new (it will default to save and send but we aren't email these receipts to anyone for this exercise, it will save your preference as the default going forward).

5. Feb 4: Jerry Kline paid $25 for a first time gym registration fee and a monthly membership fee of $35 (total received $60). (Sales Receipt)

6. Feb 4: Received bill from Yoga Bliss, LLC in the amount of $235.00 for yoga mats and towels (i.e. fitness supplies – create a new expense account – detail type Supplies & Materials) with terms of 2% 10, Net 30 (add new term 2/10, n/30 – 2% discount if paid within 10 days, net due in 30 days).

   Note: As of this writing, the option to create a term with a discount was not displayed on the Firefox browser; please use Google Chrome if possible. If not possible and the discount box is not there, use Net 30 instead.

7. Feb 4: Jim Hill paid $25 for a first time gym registration fee and a monthly membership fee of $35. (Sales Receipt)

8. Feb 4: Augusto Gutierrez paid $90 for a Quarterly Membership (i.e. 3 months of gym membership). For Quarterly memberships, the monthly rate is discounted to $30/month and the registration fee is waived because of prepayment. (Sales Receipt)

9. Feb 5: Check #1013 to Long for Success, LLC in the amount of $450.00 for QuickBooks Online setup and training (Create a new account for accounting fees as a sub-account of Legal & Professional Fees).

10. Feb 6: Sent invoices to Adrian Gonzalez, Daniel Brown, and Lucy Hopper in the amount of $35 each for February gym membership (Monthly membership) with terms of n/10 (add new terms). Their gym registration fee was waived because they signed up in advance. (Select Invoice from the Create icon, it is under the Customers section). Click Save and New after entering each invoice.

    TIP: You could send (email) the invoices to customers or make the invoice recurring (since it is a monthly membership). However, we won't do either in this practice set.

11. Feb 7: The following table lists the members who signed up and paid for February fitness classes (i.e. enter a Sales Receipt for each one). All classes are $50.

Basic Fitness 101	Wicked Weights	Kardio Killers	Yoga Fitness
Jerry Kline	Daniel Brown		
Adrian Gonzalez	Jim Hill		
Lucy Steele			

12. Feb 7: Tim Barnes paid $25 for a first time gym registration fee and a monthly membership fee of $35. (Sales Receipt)

13. Feb 7: Sold 1 hour of personal training to Tim Barnes for $35. (Sales Receipt)

14. Feb 7: Received payment of $35 from Adrian Gonzalez for February gym membership. (Received Payment is under the Customers section of the Create icon menu).

Note: For all received payment transactions, select check as the payment method and deposit to Undeposited Funds.

15. Feb 7: Total food sales from the week are shown in the table below:

Note: Add a customer named Weekly Sales and enter a Sales Receipt for the weekly sales, leave the tax box checked as you add each item.

Item	Quantity Sold	Sales Price	Totals
Bottled Water		$1.50	
Sports Drink:			
Lemon		2.00	
Orange	2	2.00	$4.00
Blue	2	2.00	4.00
Red		2.00	
Energy Drink:			
Regular		3.75	
Sugar-Free		3.75	

Nutrition Bar:			
Chocolate	1	3.25	3.25
Vanilla		3.25	
Peanut Butter		3.25	
Subtotal			**11.25**
Sales Tax			**0.79**
Total			**12.04**

16. Feb 7: Deposited all Undeposited funds from the first week of the month into the checking account by clicking Bank Deposit from the Create icon menu (under the Other section) and click select all (total deposit $662.04).

17. Feb 8: Recorded inventory adjustment: loss of 6 sugar-free energy drinks. A 6-pack of drinks was dropped and all cans were punctured.

    Note: Click the Create icon, Inventory qty adjustment under the Other section, change the date to February 8th, start typing Sugar-Free and select the item and the current quantity of 24 will be displayed, type in the new quantity of 18 and hit Save and close. Leave the inventory adjustment account as inventory shrinkage.

18. Feb 8: Check #1014 to Copper Property Management Co. in the amount of $1,500.00 for February rent.

19. Feb 10: Robert Markum paid $25 for a first time gym registration fee and a monthly membership fee of $35.

20. Feb 10: Sold 1 hour of personal training to Adrian Gonzalez for $35 (Sales Receipt).

21. Feb 11: Received payment of $35 from Lucy Hopper for February gym membership (previously invoiced).

22. Feb 12: Charged $68.97 on Visa credit card at Wal-Mart for cleaning supplies (set up a new account).

23. Feb 14: Julie Stein paid $90 for a quarterly (3 months) gym membership.

24. Feb 14: Total food sales from the week are shown in the table below:

Item	Quantity Sold	Sales Price	Totals
Bottled Water		$1.50	
Sports Drink:			
Lemon	3	2.00	$6.00
Orange		2.00	
Blue	2	2.00	4.00
Red	1	2.00	2.00
Energy Drink:			
Regular		3.75	
Sugar-Free	2	3.75	7.50
Nutrition Bar:			
Chocolate	3	3.25	9.75
Vanilla		3.25	
Peanut Butter		3.25	
Subtotal			**29.25**
Sales Tax			**2.05**
Total			**31.30**

25. Feb 14: Deposited all Undeposited funds from the second week of the month into the checking account. (Total Deposit $251.30)

26. Feb 14: Received payment of $35 from Daniel Brown for February gym membership (previously invoiced).

27. Feb 15: Paid bill from Yoga Bliss, LLC with Hand Written Check #1015 in the amount of $235 (Go to Vendors > Pay Bills and select the one from Yoga Bliss and be sure to enter the correct payment date). Since it was after 10 days from the invoice date of February 4th Fitness Haven pays the full amount (no 2% discount)

28. Feb 15: Issued a partial refund to Jim Hill for $20 because he sustained an injury and cannot use the rest of his month's membership.

Note: Select Refund Receipt under the Customer section of the Create icon menu. Enter the customer name and enter the credit for the Item of Monthly Membership and change the amount to $20. Select Check as the payment method (#1016), and the checking account under the Refund From section, and then click Save and close.

29. Feb 16: Cindy Blackburn paid $25 for a first time gym registration fee and a monthly membership fee of $35.

30. Feb 18: Received bill from Swisher Marketing, LLC in the amount of $750.00 for direct mail marketing campaign with terms of n/30. (Advertising expense)

31. Feb 20: Christopher Tomlinson paid $25 for a first time gym registration fee and a monthly membership fee of $35.

32. Feb 21: Total food sales from the week are shown in the table below:

Item	Quantity Sold	Sales Price	Totals
Bottled Water	3	$1.50	$4.50
Sports Drink:			
Lemon		2.00	
Orange	1	2.00	2.00
Blue	4	2.00	8.00
Red		2.00	
Energy Drink:			
Regular		3.75	
Sugar-Free	3	3.75	11.25
Nutrition Bar:			
Chocolate	1	3.25	3.25
Vanilla	2	3.25	6.50
Peanut Butter	1	3.25	3.25
Subtotal			**38.75**
Sales Tax			**2.40**
Total			**41.15**

33. Feb 21: Deposited all Undeposited funds from the third week of the month into the checking account. Total Deposit is $196.15.

34. Feb 22: Sent invoices to the following members in the amount of $35 for March membership (i.e. Monthly membership) with terms of n/30:

- Daniel Brown
- Adrian Gonzalez
- Lucy Steele
- Jerry Kline
- Tim Barnes
- Robert Markum
- Cindy Blackburn

Note: Lucy Hopper, Jim Hill, and Christopher Tomlinson decided to not renew their membership.

35. Feb 23: Lynn Sampson paid $90 for a quarterly gym membership.

36. Feb 25: Paid bill from Swisher Marketing, LLC. in the amount of $750.00 with check #1017.

37. Feb 26: Sold 2 hours of personal training to Adrian Gonzalez for a total of $70.

38. Feb 27: Charged $56.70 on Visa credit card at Office Depot for printer ink (office expenses).

39. Feb 27: Paid all outstanding bills. Total paid $554.41 and let QuickBooks Online assign check numbers 1018 through 1022.

40. Feb 28: Received bill from Time Warner in the amount of $147.62 for phone, internet, and cable services with terms of n/30.

41. Feb 28: Received bill from Metro Electric Co. in the amount of $178.86 for electricity with terms of n/30.

42. Feb 28: Received bill from City of Springfield in the amount of for $86.45 for water with terms of n/30.

43. Feb 28: Received bill from Waste Management in the amount of $45.00 for trash removal with terms of n/30.

44. Feb 28: Total food sales from the week are shown in the table below:

Item	Quantity Sold	Sales Price	Totals
Bottled Water	5	$1.50	$7.50
Sports Drink:			
Lemon	4	2.00	8.00
Orange	2	2.00	4.00
Blue	3	2.00	6.00
Red		2.00	
Energy Drink:			
Regular		3.75	
Sugar-Free	5	3.75	18.75
Nutrition Bar:			
Chocolate	2	3.25	6.50
Vanilla	3	3.25	9.75
Peanut Butter	1	3.25	3.25
Subtotal			**63.75**
Sales Tax			**3.94**
Total			**67.69**

45. Feb 28: Deposited all Undeposited funds from the last week of the month into the checking account. Total Deposit is $227.69.

Reconcile Accounts

Use the following information to reconcile the checking account:

Bank Statement Ending Date	2/28/2019
Bank Statement Ending Balance	$117,672.78
Outstanding Checks: Check # 1018 $147.62 Check # 1019 $183.86 Check # 1020 $51.45 Check # 1021 $45.00 Check # 1022 $126.48	Outstanding Deposits: 2/28/2019 $228.85

Use the following information to reconcile the Visa credit card account:

Statement Ending Date	2/28/2019
Statement Ending Balance	$68.97
Outstanding Items: Office Depot $56.70	

After reconciling the credit card account, select Write a check for payment now. Enter the payment date of **March 1st** payable to Great American Bank for $68.97 with check number 1023.

Check Your Progress

Create the following reports and compare them to the following reports. (Make sure to change your dates to include all of February or as of February 28th for some reports).

Balance Sheet

Fitness Haven, LLC
Balance Sheet
As of February 28, 2019

	Total
ASSETS	
Current Assets	
Bank Accounts	
Fitness Haven Checking	117,346.06
Total Bank Accounts	**$117,346.06**
Accounts Receivable	
Accounts Receivable (A/R)	245.00
Total Accounts Receivable	**$ 245.00**
Other Current Assets	
Inventory Asset	93.14
Undeposited Funds	0.00
Total Other Current Assets	**$ 93.14**
Total Current Assets	**$117,684.20**
Fixed Assets	
Fitness Equipment	
Elliptical Machines	10,000.00
Free Weights	8,000.00
Stationary Bikes	12,000.00
Treadmills	10,000.00
Weight Machines	40,000.00
Total Fitness Equipment	**$ 80,000.00**
Leasehold Improvements	52,736.89
Office Furniture and Equipment	4,123.15
Outdoor Signage	1,200.00
Total Fixed Assets	**$138,060.04**
Other Assets	
Security Deposit	3,000.00
Total Other Assets	**$ 3,000.00**

TOTAL ASSETS		$258,744.24
LIABILITIES AND EQUITY		
Liabilities		
Current Liabilities		
Accounts Payable		
Accounts Payable (A/P)		457.93
Total Accounts Payable	$	457.93
Credit Cards		
Visa		125.67
Total Credit Cards	$	125.67
Other Current Liabilities		
Iowa Department of Revenue Payable		9.18
Total Other Current Liabilities	$	9.18
Total Current Liabilities	$	592.78
Long-Term Liabilities		
Note Payable - Hometown Bank		250,000.00
Total Long-Term Liabilities		$250,000.00
Total Liabilities		$250,592.78
Equity		
Joe Watson		
Joe Partner Contributions		5,000.00
Total Joe Watson	$	5,000.00
Nancy Clemens		
Nancy Partner Contributions		5,000.00
Total Nancy Clemens	$	5,000.00
Opening Balance Equity		0.00
Retained Earnings		
Tom Martin		
Tom Partner Contributions		5,000.00
Total Tom Martin	$	5,000.00
Net Income		-6,848.54
Total Equity	$	8,151.46
TOTAL LIABILITIES AND EQUITY		$258,744.24

Profit & Loss (Jan 01 - Feb 28)

To create a monthly Profit & Loss, go to Reports > Profit & Loss and change the dates from 1/1 to 2/28 and change Display columns by from Total Only to Months and then click Run report.

Fitness Haven, LLC
Profit and Loss
January - February, 2019

	Jan 2019	Feb 2019	Total
Income			
Gym Revenues		1,235.00	1,235.00
Registration Fees		175.00	175.00
Sales of Product Income		143.00	143.00
Total Income	$ 0.00	$ 1,553.00	$ 1,553.00
Cost of Goods Sold			
Cost of Goods Sold		27.04	27.04
Inventory Shrinkage		6.30	6.30
Total Cost of Goods Sold	$ 0.00	$ 33.34	$ 33.34
Gross Profit	$ 0.00	$ 1,519.66	$ 1,519.66
Expenses			
Advertising & Marketing	225.00	900.00	1,125.00
Cleaning Supplies		68.97	68.97
Computer and Internet Expense	550.00		550.00
Fitness Supplies		235.00	235.00
Legal & Professional Services	1,785.00		1,785.00
Accounting Fees		450.00	450.00
Total Legal & Professional Services	$ 1,785.00	$ 450.00	$ 2,235.00
Office Supplies & Software	136.67	56.70	193.37
Rent & Lease	1,500.00	1,500.00	3,000.00
Repairs & Maintenance		75.00	75.00
Utilities			0.00
Electric	183.86	178.86	362.72
Phone/Internet	147.62	147.62	295.24
Trash	45.00	45.00	90.00
Water	51.45	86.45	137.90
Total Utilities	$ 427.93	$ 457.93	$ 885.86
Total Expenses	$ 4,624.60	$ 3,743.60	$ 8,368.20
Net Operating Income	-$ 4,624.60	-$ 2,223.94	-$ 6,848.54
Net Income	-$ 4,624.60	-$ 2,223.94	-$ 6,848.54

Accounts Receivable (A/R) Aging Detail

Fitness Haven, LLC
A/R Aging Detail
As of February 28, 2019

	Date	Transaction Type	Num	Customer	Due Date	Amount	Open Balance
Current							
	02/22/2019	Invoice	1024	Daniel Brown	03/24/2019	35.00	35.00
	02/22/2019	Invoice	1025	Adrian Gonzalez	03/24/2019	35.00	35.00
	02/22/2019	Invoice	1026	Lucy Steele	03/24/2019	35.00	35.00
	02/22/2019	Invoice	1027	Jerry Kline	03/24/2019	35.00	35.00
	02/22/2019	Invoice	1028	Tim Barnes	03/24/2019	35.00	35.00
	02/22/2019	Invoice	1029	Robert Markum	03/24/2019	35.00	35.00
	02/22/2019	Invoice	1030	Cindy Blackburn	03/24/2019	35.00	35.00
Total for Current						**$ 245.00**	**$ 245.00**
TOTAL						**$ 245.00**	**$ 245.00**

Accounts Payable (A/P) Aging Detail

Fitness Haven, LLC
A/P Aging Detail
As of February 28, 2019

	Date	Transaction Type	Num	Vendor	Due Date	Amount	Open Balance
Current							
	02/28/2019	Bill		Metro Electric Co.	03/30/2019	178.86	178.86
	02/28/2019	Bill		Time Warner	03/30/2019	147.62	147.62
	02/28/2019	Bill		City of Springfield	03/30/2019	86.45	86.45
	02/28/2019	Bill		Waste Management	03/30/2019	45.00	45.00
Total for Current						**$ 457.93**	**$ 457.93**
TOTAL						**$ 457.93**	**$ 457.93**

QUICKBOOKS ONLINE PRACTICE SET

Sales by Customer Detail

Sales by Customer Detail
January - February, 2019

	Date	Transaction Type	Num	Product/Service	Qty	Sales Price	Amount	Balance
Adrian Gonzalez								
	02/06/2019	Invoice	1005	Monthly Membership	1	35.00	35.00	35.00
	02/07/2019	Sales Receipt	1009	Basic Fitness 101	1	50.00	50.00	85.00
	02/10/2019	Sales Receipt	1017	Personal Training	1	35.00	35.00	120.00
	02/22/2019	Invoice	1025	Monthly Membership	1	35.00	35.00	155.00
	02/26/2019	Sales Receipt	1032	Personal Training	2	35.00	70.00	225.00
Total for Adrian Gonzalez							$ 225.00	
Anthony Gutierrez								
	02/04/2019	Sales Receipt	1004	Quarterly Membership	1	90.00	90.00	90.00
Total for Anthony Gutierrez							$ 90.00	
Christopher Tomlinson								
	02/20/2019	Sales Receipt	1022	Monthly Membership	1	35.00	35.00	35.00
	02/20/2019	Sales Receipt	1022	Registration Fee	1	25.00	25.00	60.00
Total for Christopher Tomlinson							$ 60.00	
Cindy Blackburn								
	02/16/2019	Sales Receipt	1021	Registration Fee	1	25.00	25.00	25.00
	02/16/2019	Sales Receipt	1021	Monthly Membership	1	35.00	35.00	60.00
	02/22/2019	Invoice	1030	Monthly Membership	1	35.00	35.00	95.00
Total for Cindy Blackburn							$ 95.00	
Daniel Brown								
	02/06/2019	Invoice	1006	Monthly Membership	1	35.00	35.00	35.00
	02/07/2019	Sales Receipt	1011	Wicked Weights	1	50.00	50.00	85.00
	02/22/2019	Invoice	1024	Monthly Membership	1	35.00	35.00	120.00
Total for Daniel Brown							$ 120.00	
Jerry Kline								
	02/04/2019	Sales Receipt	1002	Registration Fee	1	25.00	25.00	25.00
	02/04/2019	Sales Receipt	1002	Monthly Membership	1	35.00	35.00	60.00
	02/07/2019	Sales Receipt	1008	Basic Fitness 101	1	50.00	50.00	110.00
	02/22/2019	Invoice	1027	Monthly Membership	1	35.00	35.00	145.00
Total for Jerry Kline							$ 145.00	
Jim Hill								
	02/04/2019	Sales Receipt	1003	Registration Fee	1	25.00	25.00	25.00
	02/04/2019	Sales Receipt	1003	Monthly Membership	1	35.00	35.00	60.00
	02/07/2019	Sales Receipt	1012	Wicked Weights	1	50.00	50.00	110.00
	02/15/2019	Refund	1020	Monthly Membership	-1	20.00	-20.00	90.00
Total for Jim Hill							$ 90.00	
Julie Stein								
	02/14/2019	Sales Receipt	1018	Quarterly Membership	1	90.00	90.00	90.00

43

Total for Julie Stein							**$ 90.00**	
Lucy Hopper								
	02/06/2019	Invoice	1007	Monthly Membership	1	35.00	35.00	35.00
Total for Lucy Hopper							**$ 35.00**	
Lucy Steele								
	02/04/2019	Sales Receipt	1001	Monthly Membership	1	35.00	35.00	35.00
	02/04/2019	Sales Receipt	1001	Registration Fee	1	25.00	25.00	60.00
	02/07/2019	Sales Receipt	1010	Basic Fitness 101	1	50.00	50.00	110.00
	02/22/2019	Invoice	1026	Monthly Membership	1	35.00	35.00	145.00
Total for Lucy Steele							**$ 145.00**	
Lynn Sampson								
	02/23/2019	Sales Receipt	1031	Quarterly Membership	1	90.00	90.00	90.00
Total for Lynn Sampson							**$ 90.00**	
Robert Markum								
	02/10/2019	Sales Receipt	1016	Monthly Membership	1	35.00	35.00	35.00
	02/10/2019	Sales Receipt	1016	Registration Fee	1	25.00	25.00	60.00
	02/22/2019	Invoice	1029	Monthly Membership	1	35.00	35.00	95.00
Total for Robert Markum							**$ 95.00**	
Tim Barnes								
	02/07/2019	Sales Receipt	1014	Personal Training	1	35.00	35.00	35.00
	02/07/2019	Sales Receipt	1013	Monthly Membership	1	35.00	35.00	70.00
	02/07/2019	Sales Receipt	1013	Registration Fee	1	25.00	25.00	95.00
	02/22/2019	Invoice	1028	Monthly Membership	1	35.00	35.00	130.00
Total for Tim Barnes							**$ 130.00**	
Weekly Sales								
	02/07/2019	Sales Receipt	1015	Sports Drink:Blue	2	2.00	4.00	4.00
	02/07/2019	Sales Receipt	1015	Sports Drink:Orange	2	2.00	4.00	8.00
	02/07/2019	Sales Receipt	1015	Nutrition Bar:Chocolate	1	3.25	3.25	11.25
	02/14/2019	Sales Receipt	1019	Energy Drink:Sugar-Free	2	3.75	7.50	18.75
	02/14/2019	Sales Receipt	1019	Sports Drink:Red	1	2.00	2.00	20.75
	02/14/2019	Sales Receipt	1019	Sports Drink:Blue	2	2.00	4.00	24.75
	02/14/2019	Sales Receipt	1019	Sports Drink:Lemon	3	2.00	6.00	30.75
	02/14/2019	Sales Receipt	1019	Nutrition Bar:Chocolate	3	3.25	9.75	40.50
	02/21/2019	Sales Receipt	1023	Nutrition Bar:Vanilla	2	3.25	6.50	47.00
	02/21/2019	Sales Receipt	1023	Bottled Water	3	1.50	4.50	51.50
	02/21/2019	Sales Receipt	1023	Sports Drink:Orange	1	2.00	2.00	53.50
	02/21/2019	Sales Receipt	1023	Sports Drink:Blue	4	2.00	8.00	61.50
	02/21/2019	Sales Receipt	1023	Energy Drink:Sugar-Free	3	3.75	11.25	72.75
	02/21/2019	Sales Receipt	1023	Nutrition Bar:Chocolate	1	3.25	3.25	76.00
	02/21/2019	Sales Receipt	1023	Nutrition Bar:Peanut Butter	1	3.25	3.25	79.25
	02/28/2019	Sales Receipt	1033	Nutrition Bar:Vanilla	3	3.25	9.75	89.00
	02/28/2019	Sales Receipt	1033	Nutrition Bar:Chocolate	2	3.25	6.50	95.50
	02/28/2019	Sales Receipt	1033	Energy Drink:Sugar-Free	5	3.75	18.75	114.25
	02/28/2019	Sales Receipt	1033	Sports Drink:Red	3	2.00	6.00	120.25
	02/28/2019	Sales Receipt	1033	Sports Drink:Orange	2	2.00	4.00	124.25

Date	Transaction Type	Num	Customer	Qty	Sales Price	Amount	Balance
02/28/2019	Sales Receipt	1033	Sports Drink:Lemon	4	2.00	8.00	132.25
02/28/2019	Sales Receipt	1033	Nutrition Bar:Peanut Butter	1	3.25	3.25	135.50
02/28/2019	Sales Receipt	1033	Bottled Water	5	1.50	7.50	143.00

Total for Weekly Sales   **$ 143.00**

TOTAL   **$ 1,553.00**

Sales by Product/Service Detail

Fitness Haven, LLC
Sales by Product/Service Detail
January - February, 2019

Date	Transaction Type	Num	Customer	Qty	Sales Price	Amount	Balance
Basic Fitness 101							
02/07/2019	Sales Receipt	1008	Jerry Kline	1	50.00	50.00	50.00
02/07/2019	Sales Receipt	1010	Lucy Steele	1	50.00	50.00	100.00
02/07/2019	Sales Receipt	1009	Adrian Gonzalez	1	50.00	50.00	150.00
Total for Basic Fitness 101				3		$ 150.00	
Bottled Water							
02/21/2019	Sales Receipt	1023	Weekly Sales	3	1.50	4.50	4.50
02/28/2019	Sales Receipt	1033	Weekly Sales	5	1.50	7.50	12.00
Total for Bottled Water				8		$ 12.00	
Energy Drink							
Sugar-Free							
02/14/2019	Sales Receipt	1019	Weekly Sales	2	3.75	7.50	7.50
02/21/2019	Sales Receipt	1023	Weekly Sales	3	3.75	11.25	18.75
02/28/2019	Sales Receipt	1033	Weekly Sales	5	3.75	18.75	37.50
Total for Sugar-Free				10		$ 37.50	
Total for Energy Drink				10		$ 37.50	
Monthly Membership							
02/04/2019	Sales Receipt	1003	Jim Hill	1	35.00	35.00	35.00
02/04/2019	Sales Receipt	1002	Jerry Kline	1	35.00	35.00	70.00
02/04/2019	Sales Receipt	1001	Lucy Steele	1	35.00	35.00	105.00
02/06/2019	Invoice	1006	Daniel Brown	1	35.00	35.00	140.00
02/06/2019	Invoice	1005	Adrian Gonzalez	1	35.00	35.00	175.00
02/06/2019	Invoice	1007	Lucy Hopper	1	35.00	35.00	210.00
02/07/2019	Sales Receipt	1013	Tim Barnes	1	35.00	35.00	245.00
02/10/2019	Sales Receipt	1016	Robert Markum	1	35.00	35.00	280.00
02/15/2019	Refund	1020	Jim Hill	-1	20.00	-20.00	260.00
02/16/2019	Sales Receipt	1021	Cindy Blackburn	1	35.00	35.00	295.00

02/20/2019	Sales Receipt	1022	Christopher Tomlinson	1	35.00	35.00	330.00
02/22/2019	Invoice	1026	Lucy Steele	1	35.00	35.00	365.00
02/22/2019	Invoice	1024	Daniel Brown	1	35.00	35.00	400.00
02/22/2019	Invoice	1029	Robert Markum	1	35.00	35.00	435.00
02/22/2019	Invoice	1025	Adrian Gonzalez	1	35.00	35.00	470.00
02/22/2019	Invoice	1027	Jerry Kline	1	35.00	35.00	505.00
02/22/2019	Invoice	1028	Tim Barnes	1	35.00	35.00	540.00
02/22/2019	Invoice	1030	Cindy Blackburn	1	35.00	35.00	575.00

Total for Monthly Membership — 16 — $ 575.00

Nutrition Bar

  Chocolate

02/07/2019	Sales Receipt	1015	Weekly Sales	1	3.25	3.25	3.25
02/14/2019	Sales Receipt	1019	Weekly Sales	3	3.25	9.75	13.00
02/21/2019	Sales Receipt	1023	Weekly Sales	1	3.25	3.25	16.25
02/28/2019	Sales Receipt	1033	Weekly Sales	2	3.25	6.50	22.75

  Total for Chocolate — 7 — $ 22.75

  Peanut Butter

02/21/2019	Sales Receipt	1023	Weekly Sales	1	3.25	3.25	3.25
02/28/2019	Sales Receipt	1033	Weekly Sales	1	3.25	3.25	6.50

  Total for Peanut Butter — 2 — $ 6.50

  Vanilla

02/21/2019	Sales Receipt	1023	Weekly Sales	2	3.25	6.50	6.50
02/28/2019	Sales Receipt	1033	Weekly Sales	3	3.25	9.75	16.25

  Total for Vanilla — 5 — $ 16.25

Total for Nutrition Bar — 14 — $ 45.50

Personal Training

02/07/2019	Sales Receipt	1014	Tim Barnes	1	35.00	35.00	35.00
02/10/2019	Sales Receipt	1017	Adrian Gonzalez	1	35.00	35.00	70.00
02/26/2019	Sales Receipt	1032	Adrian Gonzalez	2	35.00	70.00	140.00

Total for Personal Training — 4 — $ 140.00

Quarterly Membership

02/04/2019	Sales Receipt	1004	Anthony Gutierrez	1	90.00	90.00	90.00
02/14/2019	Sales Receipt	1018	Julie Stein	1	90.00	90.00	180.00
02/23/2019	Sales Receipt	1031	Lynn Sampson	1	90.00	90.00	270.00

Total for Quarterly Membership — 3 — $ 270.00

Registration Fee

02/04/2019	Sales Receipt	1001	Lucy Steele	1	25.00	25.00	25.00
02/04/2019	Sales Receipt	1002	Jerry Kline	1	25.00	25.00	50.00
02/04/2019	Sales Receipt	1003	Jim Hill	1	25.00	25.00	75.00
02/07/2019	Sales Receipt	1013	Tim Barnes	1	25.00	25.00	100.00
02/10/2019	Sales Receipt	1016	Robert Markum	1	25.00	25.00	125.00
02/16/2019	Sales Receipt	1021	Cindy Blackburn	1	25.00	25.00	150.00
02/20/2019	Sales Receipt	1022	Christopher Tomlinson	1	25.00	25.00	175.00

Total for Registration Fee					**7**		**$ 175.00**	
Sports Drink								
Blue								
	02/07/2019	Sales Receipt	1015	Weekly Sales	2	2.00	4.00	4.00
	02/14/2019	Sales Receipt	1019	Weekly Sales	2	2.00	4.00	8.00
	02/21/2019	Sales Receipt	1023	Weekly Sales	4	2.00	8.00	16.00
Total for Blue					**8**		**$ 16.00**	
Lemon								
	02/14/2019	Sales Receipt	1019	Weekly Sales	3	2.00	6.00	6.00
	02/28/2019	Sales Receipt	1033	Weekly Sales	4	2.00	8.00	14.00
Total for Lemon					**7**		**$ 14.00**	
Orange								
	02/07/2019	Sales Receipt	1015	Weekly Sales	2	2.00	4.00	4.00
	02/21/2019	Sales Receipt	1023	Weekly Sales	1	2.00	2.00	6.00
	02/28/2019	Sales Receipt	1033	Weekly Sales	2	2.00	4.00	10.00
Total for Orange					**5**		**$ 10.00**	
Red								
	02/14/2019	Sales Receipt	1019	Weekly Sales	1	2.00	2.00	2.00
	02/28/2019	Sales Receipt	1033	Weekly Sales	3	2.00	6.00	8.00
Total for Red					**4**		**$ 8.00**	
Total for Sports Drink					**24**		**$ 48.00**	
Wicked Weights								
	02/07/2019	Sales Receipt	1011	Daniel Brown	1	50.00	50.00	50.00
	02/07/2019	Sales Receipt	1012	Jim Hill	1	50.00	50.00	100.00
Total for Wicked Weights					**2**		**$ 100.00**	
TOTAL					**91**		**$1,553.00**	

Inventory Valuation Summary

Fitness Haven, LLC
Inventory Valuation Summary
As of February 28, 2019

	SKU	Qty	Asset Value	Calc. Avg
Bottled Water		40.00	6.80	0.17
Energy Drink				
Regular		24.00	25.20	1.05
Sugar-Free		8.00	8.40	1.05
Total Energy Drink			$ 33.60	
Nutrition Bar				
Chocolate		17.00	7.65	0.45
Peanut Butter		22.00	9.90	0.45
Vanilla		19.00	8.55	0.45
Total Nutrition Bar			$ 26.10	
Sports Drink				
Blue		16.00	5.92	0.37
Lemon		17.00	6.29	0.37
Orange		19.00	7.03	0.37
Red		20.00	7.40	0.37
Sugar-Free		0.00	0.00	
Total Sports Drink			$ 26.64	
TOTAL			$ 93.14	

Transaction List by Date

Fitness Haven, LLC
Transaction List by Date
February 2019

Date	Transaction Type	Num	Posting	Name	Account	Split	Amount
02/01/2019	Check	1010	Yes	Great American Bank	Fitness Haven Checking	Visa	-1,859.82
02/01/2019	Check	1011	Yes	Oak Hill Homeowners Association	Fitness Haven Checking	Advertising & Marketing	-150.00
02/03/2019	Check	1012	Yes	Willy's Windows	Fitness Haven Checking	Repairs & Maintenance	-75.00
02/03/2019	Bill		Yes	Fit Foods, Inc.	Accounts Payable (A/P)	-Split-	126.48
02/04/2019	Sales Receipt	1001	Yes	Lucy Steele	Undeposited Funds	-Split-	60.00
02/04/2019	Sales Receipt	1002	Yes	Jerry Kline	Undeposited Funds	-Split-	60.00
02/04/2019	Bill		Yes	Yoga Bliss, LLC	Accounts Payable (A/P)	Fitness Supplies	235.00
02/04/2019	Sales Receipt	1003	Yes	Jim Hill	Undeposited Funds	-Split-	60.00
02/04/2019	Sales Receipt	1004	Yes	Anthony Gutierrez	Undeposited Funds	Gym Revenues	90.00
02/04/2019	Check	1013	Yes	Long for Success, LLC	Fitness Haven Checking	Legal & Professional Services:Accounting Fees	-450.00
02/06/2019	Invoice	1005	Yes	Adrian Gonzalez	Accounts Receivable (A/R)	Gym Revenues	35.00
02/06/2019	Invoice	1006	Yes	Daniel Brown	Accounts Receivable (A/R)	Gym Revenues	35.00
02/06/2019	Invoice	1007	Yes	Lucy Hopper	Accounts Receivable (A/R)	Gym Revenues	35.00
02/07/2019	Sales Receipt	1008	Yes	Jerry Kline	Undeposited Funds	Gym Revenues	50.00
02/07/2019	Sales Receipt	1009	Yes	Adrian Gonzalez	Undeposited Funds	Gym Revenues	50.00
02/07/2019	Sales Receipt	1010	Yes	Lucy Steele	Undeposited Funds	Gym Revenues	50.00
02/07/2019	Sales Receipt	1011	Yes	Daniel Brown	Undeposited Funds	Gym Revenues	50.00
02/07/2019	Sales Receipt	1012	Yes	Jim Hill	Undeposited Funds	Gym Revenues	50.00
02/07/2019	Sales Receipt	1013	Yes	Tim Barnes	Undeposited Funds	-Split-	60.00
02/07/2019	Sales Receipt	1014	Yes	Tim Barnes	Undeposited Funds	Gym Revenues	35.00
02/07/2019	Payment		Yes	Adrian Gonzalez	Undeposited Funds	Accounts Receivable (A/R)	35.00
02/07/2019	Sales Receipt	1015	Yes	Weekly Sales	Undeposited Funds	-Split-	12.04
02/07/2019	Deposit		Yes		Fitness Haven Checking	-Split-	662.04
02/08/2019	Inventory Qty Adjust	13	Yes		Inventory Shrinkage	Inventory Asset	
02/08/2019	Check	1014	Yes	Copper Property Management Co.	Fitness Haven Checking	Rent & Lease	-1,500.00
02/10/2019	Sales Receipt	1016	Yes	Robert Markum	Undeposited Funds	-Split-	60.00
02/10/2019	Sales Receipt	1017	Yes	Adrian Gonzalez	Undeposited Funds	Gym Revenues	35.00
02/11/2019	Payment		Yes	Lucy Hopper	Undeposited Funds	Accounts Receivable (A/R)	35.00
02/12/2019	Expense		Yes	Wal-Mart	Visa	Cleaning Supplies	68.97

Date	Type	Num		Name	Account	Category	Amount
02/14/2019	Sales Receipt	1018	Yes	Julie Stein	Undeposited Funds	Gym Revenues	90.00
02/14/2019	Sales Receipt	1019	Yes	Weekly Sales	Undeposited Funds	-Split-	31.30
02/14/2019	Deposit		Yes		Fitness Haven Checking	-Split-	251.30
02/14/2019	Payment		Yes	Daniel Brown	Undeposited Funds	Accounts Receivable (A/R)	35.00
02/15/2019	Bill Payment (Check)	1015	Yes	Yoga Bliss, LLC	Fitness Haven Checking	Accounts Payable (A/P)	-235.00
02/15/2019	Refund	1020	Yes	Jim Hill	Fitness Haven Checking	Gym Revenues	-20.00
02/16/2019	Sales Receipt	1021	Yes	Cindy Blackburn	Undeposited Funds	-Split-	60.00
02/18/2019	Bill		Yes	Swisher Marketing	Accounts Payable (A/P)	Advertising & Marketing	750.00
02/20/2019	Sales Receipt	1022	Yes	Christopher Tomlinson	Undeposited Funds	-Split-	60.00
02/21/2019	Sales Receipt	1023	Yes	Weekly Sales	Undeposited Funds	-Split-	41.15
02/21/2019	Deposit		Yes		Fitness Haven Checking	-Split-	196.15
02/22/2019	Invoice	1024	Yes	Daniel Brown	Accounts Receivable (A/R)	Gym Revenues	35.00
02/22/2019	Invoice	1025	Yes	Adrian Gonzalez	Accounts Receivable (A/R)	Gym Revenues	35.00
02/22/2019	Invoice	1026	Yes	Lucy Steele	Accounts Receivable (A/R)	Gym Revenues	35.00
02/22/2019	Invoice	1027	Yes	Jerry Kline	Accounts Receivable (A/R)	Gym Revenues	35.00
02/22/2019	Invoice	1028	Yes	Tim Barnes	Accounts Receivable (A/R)	Gym Revenues	35.00
02/22/2019	Invoice	1029	Yes	Robert Markum	Accounts Receivable (A/R)	Gym Revenues	35.00
02/22/2019	Invoice	1030	Yes	Cindy Blackburn	Accounts Receivable (A/R)	Gym Revenues	35.00
02/23/2019	Sales Receipt	1031	Yes	Lynn Sampson	Undeposited Funds	Gym Revenues	90.00
02/25/2019	Bill Payment (Check)	1017	Yes	Swisher Marketing	Fitness Haven Checking	Accounts Payable (A/P)	-750.00
02/26/2019	Sales Receipt	1032	Yes	Adrian Gonzalez	Undeposited Funds	Gym Revenues	70.00
02/27/2019	Expense		Yes	Office Depot	Visa	Office Supplies & Software	56.70
02/27/2019	Bill Payment (Check)	1018	Yes	City of Springfield	Fitness Haven Checking	Accounts Payable (A/P)	-51.45
02/27/2019	Bill Payment (Check)	1019	Yes	Metro Electric Co.	Fitness Haven Checking	Accounts Payable (A/P)	-183.86
02/27/2019	Bill Payment (Check)	1020	Yes	Time Warner	Fitness Haven Checking	Accounts Payable (A/P)	-147.62
02/27/2019	Bill Payment (Check)	1021	Yes	Waste Management	Fitness Haven Checking	Accounts Payable (A/P)	-45.00
02/27/2019	Bill Payment (Check)	1022	Yes	Fit Foods, Inc.	Fitness Haven Checking	Accounts Payable (A/P)	-126.48
02/28/2019	Bill		Yes	Time Warner	Accounts Payable (A/P)	Utilities:Phone/Internet	147.62
02/28/2019	Bill		Yes	Metro Electric Co.	Accounts Payable (A/P)	Utilities:Electric	178.86
02/28/2019	Bill		Yes	City of Springfield	Accounts Payable (A/P)	Utilities:Water	86.45
02/28/2019	Bill		Yes	Waste Management	Accounts Payable (A/P)	Utilities:Trash	45.00
02/28/2019	Sales Receipt	1033	Yes	Weekly Sales	Undeposited Funds	-Split-	67.69
02/28/2019	Deposit		Yes		Fitness Haven Checking	-Split-	227.69

5 ENTERING TRANSACTIONS – MARCH

Notes for entering transactions:

- Use Accounts Payable (i.e. Enter Bills and Pay Bills) for monthly expenses and bills (when transactions say Received Bill and Pay Bills).

- Enter Checks as indicated for purchases from local retailers and others.

- Use a Sales Receipt for initial registration fees and membership dues received. Subsequent membership dues will be entered as an Invoice and then Receive Payment.

- Enter Sales Receipts for classes and personal training sessions.

- Payments received should go to Undeposited Funds -- you will be told when to Record Deposits.

- Do not worry about depreciation on fixed assets. We assumed the accountant or tax professional maintains details of fixed assets and depreciation.

March Transactions

1. Mar 1: Jules Silverstein paid $90 for a quarterly gym membership.

2. Mar 1: Sold 1 hour of personal training to Lynn Sampson for $35.

3. Mar 2: Received bill from Cool T-shirts Co. in the amount of $45.00 for custom staff t-shirts (set up a new expense account called uniforms, detail type office/general administrative), with terms of n/10.

4. Mar 3: Jim Dean paid $90 for a quarterly membership and 1 hour of personal training for $35 (Total Sales Receipt of $125).

5. Mar 3: Allison Hoch paid $90 for a quarterly gym membership.

6. Mar 3: Katie Layton paid $25 for a first time gym registration fee and a monthly membership fee of $35.

7. Mar 4: Received payment of $35 from Lucy Steele for March gym membership.

8. Mar 4: Recorded inventory adjustment: Fitness Haven, LLC gave out 1 free water to the first 10 customers (New Quantity on Hand is 30).

   Note: Go to the create icon and click Inventory qty adjustment, enter the date and new quantity. The old quantity should populate as 40 and enter the new quantity of 30. An adjustment will be posted to inventory and inventory shrinkage as of March 4th.

9. Mar 4: Hugo Reyson paid $90 for a quarterly gym membership.

10. Mar 6: Check #1024 to Copper Property Management Co. in the amount of $1,500.00 for March rent.

11. Mar 7: The following table lists the members who signed up and paid (Sales Receipts) for March fitness classes. All classes are $50.

Basic Fitness 101	Wicked Weights	Kardio Killers	Yoga Fitness
Allison Hoch	John Brown	Jerry Kline	Cindy Blackburn
Jim Dean	Tim Barnes	Adrian Gonzalez	Jules Silverstein
		Lucy Steele	

12. Mar 7: Total food sales from the week are shown in the table below.

Item	Quantity Sold	Sales Price	Totals
Bottled Water	7	$1.50	$10.50
Sports Drink:			
Lemon		2.00	
Orange	4	2.00	8.00
Blue	2	2.00	4.00
Red	3	2.00	6.00
Energy Drink:			
Regular		3.75	
Sugar-Free	4	3.75	15.00
Nutrition Bar:			
Chocolate	5	3.25	16.25
Vanilla		3.25	
Peanut Butter	3	3.25	9.75
Subtotal			**69.50**
Sales Tax			**4.13**
Total			**73.63**

13. Mar 7: Deposited all Undeposited funds from the first week of the month into the checking account for a total of $1,048.63.

14. Mar 8: Richard Halpert paid $90 for a quarterly gym membership.

15. Mar 9: Check #1025 to Cody's Cleaning Co. in the amount of $250.00 for a complete gym cleaning (Janitorial Expense – Office/General Administrative type expense).

16. Mar 10: John Lockhart paid $25 for a first time gym registration fee and a monthly membership fee of $35.

17. Mar 10: Received payment of $35 from Robert Markum for March gym membership.

18. Mar 11: Paid bill from Cool T-shirts Co. with check #1026 in the amount of $45 (Make sure to change the date).

19. Mar 11: Purchase order #1002 to Fit Foods, Inc. in the amount of $91.86 to purchase the following inventory items (edit for the quantities ordered below):

Item	Quantity	Unit Cost	Total Cost	Sales Price
Bottled Water	48	$0.17	$8.16	$1.50
Sports Drink:				
Lemon	12	0.37	4.44	2.00
Orange	24	0.37	8.88	2.00
Blue	48	0.37	17.76	2.00
Red	6	0.37	2.22	2.00
Energy Drink:				
Regular	24	1.05	25.20	3.75
Sugar-Free	6	1.05	6.30	3.75
Nutrition Bar:				
Chocolate	24	0.45	10.80	3.25
Vanilla	12	0.45	5.40	3.25
Peanut Butter	6	0.45	2.70	3.25

20. Mar 11: Jack Sheppert paid $90 for a quarterly gym membership.

21. Mar 12: Received payment of $35 each from Daniel Brown and Adrian Gonzalez for March gym membership.

22. Mar 13: Kate Austino paid $25 for a first time gym registration fee and a monthly membership fee of $35.

23. Mar 14: Total food sales from the week are shown in the table below:

Item	Quantity Sold	Sales Price	Totals
Bottled Water	3	$1.50	$4.50
Sports Drink:			
Lemon	2	2.00	4.00
Orange		2.00	
Blue	1	2.00	2.00
Red	2	2.00	4.00
Energy Drink:			
Regular		3.75	
Sugar-Free	2	3.75	7.50
Nutrition Bar:			
Chocolate	1	3.25	3.25
Vanilla	1	3.25	3.25
Peanut Butter		3.25	
Subtotal			**28.50**
Sales Tax			**1.68**
Total			**30.18**

24. Mar 14: Deposited all Undeposited funds from the second week of the month into the checking account for a total of $435.18.

25. Mar 16: Received payment of $35 from Cindy Blackburn for March gym membership.

26. Mar 17: Sold 1 hour of personal training to Cindy Blackburn and Jim Dean for $35 each.

27. Mar 18: Jim Sawyer paid $25 for a first time gym registration fee and a monthly membership fee of $35.

28. Mar 19: Christian Sheppert paid $90 for a quarterly gym membership.

29. Mar 20: Sold 1 hour of personal training to Kate Austino for $35.

30. Mar 20: Received payment of $35 each from Jerry Kline and Tim Barnes for March gym membership.

31. Mar 21: Danielle Russell paid $25 for a first time gym registration fee and a monthly membership fee of $35.

32. Mar 21: Total food sales from the week are shown below:

Item	Quantity Sold	Sales Price	Totals
Bottled Water	5	$1.50	7.50
Sports Drink:			
Lemon		2.00	
Orange	2	2.00	4.00
Blue	3	2.00	6.00
Red	1	2.00	2.00
Energy Drink:			
Regular	3	3.75	
Sugar-Free		3.75	11.25
Nutrition Bar:			
Chocolate	3	3.25	9.75
Vanilla	1	3.25	3.25
Peanut Butter	2	3.25	6.50
Subtotal			**50.25**
Sales Tax			**2.99**
Total			**53.24**

33. Mar 21: Deposited all Undeposited funds from the third week of the month into the checking account for a total of $473.24.

34. Mar 22: Received partial inventory from purchase order #1002 from Fit Foods, Inc. Red sports drink was not available because it has been discontinued and Vanilla Energy Bars were out of stock. Enter the bill for the receipt of all other items on the purchase for a total of $84.24. The terms are n/30.

    Note: Enter a Bill and select Fit Foods which may recall the last bill for them. If there are items and amounts already listed, click on Clear All Lines (below item details, not the clear button at the very bottom that would clear the entire transaction). Then, click to add the purchase order on the right sidebar and delete the Red Sports Drink and Vanilla Nutrition Bars items by clicking the trash can delete icon on the end of the item row (by the amount column). Click Remove line at the prompt for both (do not click the Unlink it button). The total should be $84.24.

35. Mar 24: Benny Linus paid $25 for a first time gym registration fee and a monthly membership fee of $35.

36. Mar 25: Issued a refund of $35 to Benny Linus who canceled his membership because he decided working out is too hard. (The refund was for the 1 month membership Benny purchased. The registration fee is non-refundable.) Write check #1027 for the refund.

    Note: Use the Refund Receipt choice under the Create icon menu.

37. Mar 26: Sent invoices to the following members in the amount of $35 for April membership (Monthly membership) with terms of n/30:

    - Adrian Gonzalez
    - Lucy Steele
    - Tim Barnes
    - Robert Markum
    - Katie Layton
    - John Lockhart
    - Kate Austino
    - Jim Sawyer

    Note: Jerry Kline, Daniel Brown, Cindy Blackburn, and Danielle Russell decided not to renew their membership.

38. Mar 27: Check #1028 to Rob's Repairs in the amount of $220.00 for repairing 2 broken machines.

39. Mar 28: Sold 2 hours of personal training to Adrian Gonzalez for $70.

40. Mar 30: Paid all bills for a total of $542.17 (assign check numbers 1029 to 1033 and enter correct payment date).

41. Mar 31: Received bill from Time Warner in the amount of $147.62 for phone, internet, and cable services with terms of n/30.

42. Mar 31: Received bill from Metro Electric Co. in the amount of $128.86 for electricity with terms of n/30.

43. Mar 31: Received bill from City of Springfield in the amount of for $79.45 for water with terms of n/30.

44. Mar 31: Received bill from Waste Management in the amount of $45.00 for trash removal with terms of n/30.

45. Mar 31: Total food sales from the week are shown in the table below:

Item	Quantity Sold	Sales Price	Totals
Bottled Water	10	$1.50	15.00
Sports Drink:			
Lemon	3	2.00	6.00
Orange	3	2.00	6.00
Blue	5	2.00	10.00
Red		2.00	
Energy Drink:			
Regular	5	3.75	18.75
Sugar-Free	2	3.75	7.50
Nutrition Bar:			
Chocolate	2	3.25	6.50
Vanilla	2	3.25	6.50
Peanut Butter	4	3.25	13.00
Subtotal			**89.25**
Sales Tax			**5.20**
Total			**94.45**

46. Mar 31: Deposited all Undeposited funds into the checking account for a total of $224.45.

Reconcile Accounts

Use the following information to reconcile the checking account:

Bank Statement Ending Date	3/31/2019
Bank Statement Ending Balance	$117,404.14
Outstanding Checks: Check # 1028 $220.00 Check # 1029 $147.62 Check # 1030 $178.86 Check # 1031 $86.45 Check # 1032 $45.00 Check #1033 $84.24	Outstanding Deposits: 3/31/2019 $224.45

Use the following information to reconcile the Visa credit card account:

Statement Ending Date	3/31/2019
Statement Ending Balance	$56.70
Outstanding Items: None	

After reconciling the credit card account, select the option to pay all of a portion of the bill now. Enter the payment date of **April 1st**, payable to Great American Bank with check number 1034 (should be for $56.70).

Check Your Results

Create the following reports and compare them to the following reports. (Make sure to set the dates for March)

Balance Sheet

Fitness Haven, LLC
Balance Sheet
As of March 31, 2019

	Total
ASSETS	
Current Assets	
Bank Accounts	
Fitness Haven Checking	116,866.42
Total Bank Accounts	$ 116,866.42
Accounts Receivable	
Accounts Receivable (A/R)	280.00
Total Accounts Receivable	$ 280.00
Other Current Assets	
Inventory Asset	132.36
Undeposited Funds	0.00
Total Other Current Assets	$ 132.36
Total Current Assets	$ 117,278.78
Fixed Assets	
Fitness Equipment	
Elliptical Machines	10,000.00
Free Weights	8,000.00
Stationary Bikes	12,000.00
Treadmills	10,000.00
Weight Machines	40,000.00
Total Fitness Equipment	$ 80,000.00
Leasehold Improvements	52,736.89
Office Furniture and Equipment	4,123.15
Outdoor Signage	1,200.00
Total Fixed Assets	$ 138,060.04
Other Assets	
Security Deposit	3,000.00
Total Other Assets	$ 3,000.00
TOTAL ASSETS	$ 258,338.82
LIABILITIES AND EQUITY	
Liabilities	

Current Liabilities		
Accounts Payable		
Accounts Payable (A/P)		400.93
Total Accounts Payable	$	400.93
Credit Cards		
Visa		56.70
Total Credit Cards	$	56.70
Other Current Liabilities		
Iowa Department of Revenue Payable		23.18
Total Other Current Liabilities	$	23.18
Total Current Liabilities	$	480.81
Long-Term Liabilities		
Note Payable - Hometown Bank		250,000.00
Total Long-Term Liabilities	$	250,000.00
Total Liabilities	$	250,480.81
Equity		
Joe Watson		
Joe Partner Contributions		5,000.00
Total Joe Watson	$	5,000.00
Nancy Clemens		
Nancy Partner Contributions		5,000.00
Total Nancy Clemens	$	5,000.00
Opening Balance Equity		0.00
Retained Earnings		
Tom Martin		
Tom Partner Contributions		5,000.00
Total Tom Martin	$	5,000.00
Net Income		-7,141.99
Total Equity	$	7,858.01
TOTAL LIABILITIES AND EQUITY	$	258,338.82

Profit & Loss (Jan 01 - Mar 31)

Fitness Haven, LLC
Profit and Loss
January - March, 2019

	Jan 2019	Feb 2019	Mar 2019	Total
Income				
Gym Revenues		1,235.00	1,780.00	3,015.00
Registration Fees		175.00	150.00	325.00
Sales of Product Income		143.00	237.50	380.50
Total Income	$ 0.00	$ 1,553.00	$2,167.50	$ 3,720.50
Cost of Goods Sold				
Cost of Goods Sold		27.04	43.32	70.36
Inventory Shrinkage		6.30	1.70	8.00
Total Cost of Goods Sold	$ 0.00	$ 33.34	$ 45.02	$ 78.36
Gross Profit	$ 0.00	$ 1,519.66	$2,122.48	$ 3,642.14
Expenses				
Advertising & Marketing	225.00	900.00		1,125.00
Cleaning Supplies		68.97		68.97
Computer and Internet Expense	550.00			550.00
Fitness Supplies		235.00		235.00
Janitorial Expense			250.00	250.00
Legal & Professional Services	1,785.00			1,785.00
Accounting Fees		450.00		450.00
Total Legal & Professional Services	$ 1,785.00	$ 450.00	$ 0.00	$ 2,235.00
Office Supplies & Software	136.67	56.70		193.37
Rent & Lease	1,500.00	1,500.00	1,500.00	4,500.00
Repairs & Maintenance		75.00	220.00	295.00
Uniforms			45.00	45.00
Utilities				0.00
Electric	183.86	178.86	128.86	491.58
Phone/Internet	147.62	147.62	147.62	442.86
Trash	45.00	45.00	45.00	135.00
Water	51.45	86.45	79.45	217.35
Total Utilities	$ 427.93	$ 457.93	$ 400.93	$ 1,286.79
Total Expenses	$ 4,624.60	$ 3,743.60	$2,415.93	$ 10,784.13
Net Operating Income	-$ 4,624.60	-$ 2,223.94	-$ 293.45	-$ 7,141.99
Net Income	-$ 4,624.60	-$ 2,223.94	-$ 293.45	-$ 7,141.99

Accounts Receivable (A/R) Aging Detail

Fitness Haven, LLC
A/R Aging Detail
As of March 31, 2019

Date	Transaction Type	Num	Customer	Due Date	Amount	Open Balance
Current						
03/26/2019	Invoice	1064	Adrian Gonzalez	04/25/2019	35.00	35.00
03/26/2019	Invoice	1065	Lucy Steele	04/25/2019	35.00	35.00
03/26/2019	Invoice	1066	Tim Barnes	04/25/2019	35.00	35.00
03/26/2019	Invoice	1067	Robert Markum	04/25/2019	35.00	35.00
03/26/2019	Invoice	1068	Katie Layton	04/25/2019	35.00	35.00
03/26/2019	Invoice	1069	John Lockhart	04/25/2019	35.00	35.00
03/26/2019	Invoice	1070	Kate Austino	04/25/2019	35.00	35.00
03/26/2019	Invoice	1071	Jim Sawyer	04/25/2019	35.00	35.00
Total for Current					$ 280.00	$ 280.00
TOTAL					$ 280.00	$ 280.00

Accounts Payable (A/P) Aging Detail

Fitness Haven, LLC
A/P Aging Detail
As of March 31, 2019

Date	Transaction Type	Num	Vendor	Due Date	Amount	Open Balance
Current						
03/31/2019	Bill		Time Warner	04/30/2019	147.62	147.62
03/31/2019	Bill		Metro Electric Co.	04/30/2019	128.86	128.86
03/31/2019	Bill		City of Springfield	04/30/2019	79.45	79.45
03/31/2019	Bill		Waste Management	04/30/2019	45.00	45.00
Total for Current					$ 400.93	$ 400.93
TOTAL					$ 400.93	$ 400.93

Sales by Customer Detail

Fitness Haven, LLC
Sales by Customer Detail
March 2019

	Date	Transaction Type	Num	Product/Service	Qty	Sales Price	Amount	Balance
Adrian Gonzalez								
	03/07/2019	Sales Receipt	1045	Kardio Killers	1	50.00	50.00	50.00
	03/26/2019	Invoice	1064	Monthly Membership	1	35.00	35.00	85.00
	03/28/2019	Sales Receipt	1072	Personal Training	2	35.00	70.00	155.00
Total for Adrian Gonzalez							$ 155.00	
Allison Hoch								
	03/03/2019	Sales Receipt	1037	Quarterly Membership	1	90.00	90.00	90.00
	03/07/2019	Sales Receipt	1040	Basic Fitness 101	1	50.00	50.00	140.00
Total for Allison Hoch							$ 140.00	
Benny Linus								
	03/24/2019	Sales Receipt	1062	Registration Fee	1	25.00	25.00	25.00
	03/24/2019	Sales Receipt	1062	Monthly Membership	1	35.00	35.00	60.00
	03/25/2019	Refund	1063	Monthly Membership	-1	35.00	-35.00	25.00
Total for Benny Linus							$ 25.00	
Christian Sheppert								
	03/19/2019	Sales Receipt	1058	Quarterly Membership	1	90.00	90.00	90.00
Total for Christian Sheppert							$ 90.00	
Cindy Blackburn								
	03/07/2019	Sales Receipt	1047	Yoga Fitness	1	50.00	50.00	50.00
	03/17/2019	Sales Receipt	1055	Personal Training	1	35.00	35.00	85.00
Total for Cindy Blackburn							$ 85.00	
Danielle Russell								
	03/21/2019	Sales Receipt	1060	Registration Fee	1	25.00	25.00	25.00
	03/21/2019	Sales Receipt	1060	Monthly Membership	1	35.00	35.00	60.00
Total for Danielle Russell							$ 60.00	
Hugo Reyson								
	03/04/2019	Sales Receipt	1039	Quarterly Membership	1	90.00	90.00	90.00
Total for Hugo Reyson							$ 90.00	
Jack Sheppert								
	03/11/2019	Sales Receipt	1052	Quarterly Membership	1	90.00	90.00	90.00
Total for Jack Sheppert							$ 90.00	

Jerry Kline

	03/07/2019	Sales Receipt	1044	Kardio Killers	1	50.00	50.00	50.00
Total for Jerry Kline							$ **50.00**	

Jim Dean

	03/03/2019	Sales Receipt	1036	Quarterly Membership	1	90.00	90.00	90.00
	03/03/2019	Sales Receipt	1036	Personal Training	1	35.00	35.00	125.00
	03/07/2019	Sales Receipt	1041	Basic Fitness 101	1	50.00	50.00	175.00
	03/17/2019	Sales Receipt	1056	Personal Training	1	35.00	35.00	210.00
Total for Jim Dean							$ **210.00**	

Jim Sawyer

	03/18/2019	Sales Receipt	1057	Registration Fee	1	25.00	25.00	25.00
	03/18/2019	Sales Receipt	1057	Monthly Membership	1	35.00	35.00	60.00
	03/26/2019	Invoice	1071	Monthly Membership	1	35.00	35.00	95.00
Total for Jim Sawyer							$ **95.00**	

John Brown

	03/07/2019	Sales Receipt	1042	Wicked Weights	1	50.00	50.00	50.00
Total for John Brown							$ **50.00**	

John Lockhart

	03/10/2019	Sales Receipt	1051	Registration Fee	1	25.00	25.00	25.00
	03/10/2019	Sales Receipt	1051	Monthly Membership	1	35.00	35.00	60.00
	03/26/2019	Invoice	1069	Monthly Membership	1	35.00	35.00	95.00
Total for John Lockhart							$ **95.00**	

Jules Silverstein

	03/01/2019	Sales Receipt	1034	Quarterly Membership	1	90.00	90.00	90.00
	03/07/2019	Sales Receipt	1048	Yoga Fitness	1	50.00	50.00	140.00
Total for Jules Silverstein							$ **140.00**	

Kate Austino

	03/13/2019	Sales Receipt	1053	Registration Fee	1	25.00	25.00	25.00
	03/13/2019	Sales Receipt	1053	Monthly Membership	1	35.00	35.00	60.00
	03/20/2019	Sales Receipt	1059	Personal Training	1	35.00	35.00	95.00
	03/26/2019	Invoice	1070	Monthly Membership	1	35.00	35.00	130.00
Total for Kate Austino							$ **130.00**	

Katie Layton

	03/03/2019	Sales Receipt	1038	Registration Fee	1	25.00	25.00	25.00
	03/03/2019	Sales Receipt	1038	Monthly Membership	1	35.00	35.00	60.00
	03/26/2019	Invoice	1068	Monthly Membership	1	35.00	35.00	95.00
Total for Katie Layton							$ **95.00**	

Lucy Steele

	03/07/2019	Sales Receipt	1046	Kardio Killers	1	50.00	50.00	50.00
	03/26/2019	Invoice	1065	Monthly Membership	1	35.00	35.00	85.00
Total for Lucy Steele							$ **85.00**	

Lynn Sampson

	Date	Type	Num	Item	Qty	Price	Amount	Balance
	03/01/2019	Sales Receipt	1035	Monthly Membership	1	35.00	35.00	35.00
Total for Lynn Sampson							**$ 35.00**	
Richard Halpert								
	03/08/2019	Sales Receipt	1050	Quarterly Membership	1	90.00	90.00	90.00
Total for Richard Halpert							**$ 90.00**	
Robert Markum								
	03/26/2019	Invoice	1067	Monthly Membership	1	35.00	35.00	35.00
Total for Robert Markum							**$ 35.00**	
Tim Barnes								
	03/07/2019	Sales Receipt	1043	Wicked Weights	1	50.00	50.00	50.00
	03/26/2019	Invoice	1066	Monthly Membership	1	35.00	35.00	85.00
Total for Tim Barnes							**$ 85.00**	
Weekly Sales								
	03/07/2019	Sales Receipt	1049	Nutrition Bar:Chocolate	5	3.25	16.25	16.25
	03/07/2019	Sales Receipt	1049	Energy Drink:Sugar-Free	4	3.75	15.00	31.25
	03/07/2019	Sales Receipt	1049	Sports Drink:Red	3	2.00	6.00	37.25
	03/07/2019	Sales Receipt	1049	Sports Drink:Blue	2	2.00	4.00	41.25
	03/07/2019	Sales Receipt	1049	Bottled Water	7	1.50	10.50	51.75
	03/07/2019	Sales Receipt	1049	Sports Drink:Orange	4	2.00	8.00	59.75
	03/07/2019	Sales Receipt	1049	Nutrition Bar:Peanut Butter	3	3.25	9.75	69.50
	03/14/2019	Sales Receipt	1054	Nutrition Bar:Chocolate	1	3.25	3.25	72.75
	03/14/2019	Sales Receipt	1054	Energy Drink:Sugar-Free	2	3.75	7.50	80.25
	03/14/2019	Sales Receipt	1054	Sports Drink:Red	2	2.00	4.00	84.25
	03/14/2019	Sales Receipt	1054	Sports Drink:Blue	1	2.00	2.00	86.25
	03/14/2019	Sales Receipt	1054	Sports Drink:Lemon	2	2.00	4.00	90.25
	03/14/2019	Sales Receipt	1054	Bottled Water	3	1.50	4.50	94.75
	03/14/2019	Sales Receipt	1054	Nutrition Bar:Vanilla	1	3.25	3.25	98.00
	03/21/2019	Sales Receipt	1061	Nutrition Bar:Chocolate	3	3.25	9.75	107.75
	03/21/2019	Sales Receipt	1061	Bottled Water	5	1.50	7.50	115.25
	03/21/2019	Sales Receipt	1061	Sports Drink:Orange	2	2.00	4.00	119.25
	03/21/2019	Sales Receipt	1061	Sports Drink:Blue	3	2.00	6.00	125.25
	03/21/2019	Sales Receipt	1061	Sports Drink:Red	1	2.00	2.00	127.25
	03/21/2019	Sales Receipt	1061	Nutrition Bar:Peanut Butter	2	3.25	6.50	133.75
	03/21/2019	Sales Receipt	1061	Nutrition Bar:Vanilla	1	3.25	3.25	137.00
	03/21/2019	Sales Receipt	1061	Energy Drink:Regular	3	3.75	11.25	148.25
	03/31/2019	Sales Receipt	1073	Nutrition Bar:Vanilla	2	3.25	6.50	154.75
	03/31/2019	Sales Receipt	1073	Nutrition Bar:Chocolate	2	3.25	6.50	161.25
	03/31/2019	Sales Receipt	1073	Energy Drink:Sugar-Free	2	3.75	7.50	168.75
	03/31/2019	Sales Receipt	1073	Energy Drink:Regular	5	3.75	18.75	187.50
	03/31/2019	Sales Receipt	1073	Sports Drink:Blue	5	2.00	10.00	197.50

03/31/2019	Sales Receipt	1073	Sports Drink:Orange	3	2.00	6.00	203.50
03/31/2019	Sales Receipt	1073	Sports Drink:Lemon	3	2.00	6.00	209.50
03/31/2019	Sales Receipt	1073	Nutrition Bar:Peanut Butter	4	3.25	13.00	222.50
03/31/2019	Sales Receipt	1073	Bottled Water	10	1.50	15.00	237.50

Total for Weekly Sales $ 237.50

TOTAL $ 2,167.50

Sales by Product/Service Detail

Fitness Haven, LLC
Sales by Product/Service Detail
March 2019

	Date	Transaction Type	Num	Customer	Qty	Sales Price	Amount	Balance
Basic Fitness 101								
	03/07/2019	Sales Receipt	1040	Allison Hoch	1	50.00	50.00	50.00
	03/07/2019	Sales Receipt	1041	Jim Dean	1	50.00	50.00	100.00
Total for Basic Fitness 101					2		$ 100.00	
Bottled Water								
	03/07/2019	Sales Receipt	1049	Weekly Sales	7	1.50	10.50	10.50
	03/14/2019	Sales Receipt	1054	Weekly Sales	3	1.50	4.50	15.00
	03/21/2019	Sales Receipt	1061	Weekly Sales	5	1.50	7.50	22.50
	03/31/2019	Sales Receipt	1073	Weekly Sales	10	1.50	15.00	37.50
Total for Bottled Water					25		$ 37.50	
Energy Drink								
Regular								
	03/21/2019	Sales Receipt	1061	Weekly Sales	3	3.75	11.25	11.25
	03/31/2019	Sales Receipt	1073	Weekly Sales	5	3.75	18.75	30.00
Total for Regular					8		$ 30.00	
Sugar-Free								
	03/07/2019	Sales Receipt	1049	Weekly Sales	4	3.75	15.00	15.00
	03/14/2019	Sales Receipt	1054	Weekly Sales	2	3.75	7.50	22.50
	03/31/2019	Sales Receipt	1073	Weekly Sales	2	3.75	7.50	30.00
Total for Sugar-Free					8		$ 30.00	
Total for Energy Drink					16		$ 60.00	
Kardio Killers								
	03/07/2019	Sales Receipt	1046	Lucy Steele	1	50.00	50.00	50.00
	03/07/2019	Sales Receipt	1044	Jerry Kline	1	50.00	50.00	100.00
	03/07/2019	Sales Receipt	1045	Adrian Gonzalez	1	50.00	50.00	150.00
Total for Kardio Killers					3		$ 150.00	
Monthly Membership								
	03/01/2019	Sales Receipt	1035	Lynn Sampson	1	35.00	35.00	35.00
	03/03/2019	Sales Receipt	1038	Katie Layton	1	35.00	35.00	70.00
	03/10/2019	Sales Receipt	1051	John Lockhart	1	35.00	35.00	105.00
	03/13/2019	Sales Receipt	1053	Kate Austino	1	35.00	35.00	140.00
	03/18/2019	Sales Receipt	1057	Jim Sawyer	1	35.00	35.00	175.00
	03/21/2019	Sales Receipt	1060	Danielle Russell	1	35.00	35.00	210.00
	03/24/2019	Sales Receipt	1062	Benny Linus	1	35.00	35.00	245.00

	03/25/2019	Refund	1063	Benny Linus	-1	35.00	-35.00	210.00
	03/26/2019	Invoice	1070	Kate Austino	1	35.00	35.00	245.00
	03/26/2019	Invoice	1069	John Lockhart	1	35.00	35.00	280.00
	03/26/2019	Invoice	1068	Katie Layton	1	35.00	35.00	315.00
	03/26/2019	Invoice	1071	Jim Sawyer	1	35.00	35.00	350.00
	03/26/2019	Invoice	1067	Robert Markum	1	35.00	35.00	385.00
	03/26/2019	Invoice	1064	Adrian Gonzalez	1	35.00	35.00	420.00
	03/26/2019	Invoice	1065	Lucy Steele	1	35.00	35.00	455.00
	03/26/2019	Invoice	1066	Tim Barnes	1	35.00	35.00	490.00
Total for Monthly Membership					**14**		**$ 490.00**	

Nutrition Bar

Chocolate

	03/07/2019	Sales Receipt	1049	Weekly Sales	5	3.25	16.25	16.25
	03/14/2019	Sales Receipt	1054	Weekly Sales	1	3.25	3.25	19.50
	03/21/2019	Sales Receipt	1061	Weekly Sales	3	3.25	9.75	29.25
	03/31/2019	Sales Receipt	1073	Weekly Sales	2	3.25	6.50	35.75
Total for Chocolate					**11**		**$ 35.75**	

Peanut Butter

	03/07/2019	Sales Receipt	1049	Weekly Sales	3	3.25	9.75	9.75
	03/21/2019	Sales Receipt	1061	Weekly Sales	2	3.25	6.50	16.25
	03/31/2019	Sales Receipt	1073	Weekly Sales	4	3.25	13.00	29.25
Total for Peanut Butter					**9**		**$ 29.25**	

Vanilla

	03/14/2019	Sales Receipt	1054	Weekly Sales	1	3.25	3.25	3.25
	03/21/2019	Sales Receipt	1061	Weekly Sales	1	3.25	3.25	6.50
	03/31/2019	Sales Receipt	1073	Weekly Sales	2	3.25	6.50	13.00
Total for Vanilla					**4**		**$ 13.00**	
Total for Nutrition Bar					**24**		**$ 78.00**	

Personal Training

	03/03/2019	Sales Receipt	1036	Jim Dean	1	35.00	35.00	35.00
	03/17/2019	Sales Receipt	1056	Jim Dean	1	35.00	35.00	70.00
	03/17/2019	Sales Receipt	1055	Cindy Blackburn	1	35.00	35.00	105.00
	03/20/2019	Sales Receipt	1059	Kate Austino	1	35.00	35.00	140.00
	03/28/2019	Sales Receipt	1072	Adrian Gonzalez	2	35.00	70.00	210.00
Total for Personal Training					**6**		**$ 210.00**	

Quarterly Membership

	03/01/2019	Sales Receipt	1034	Jules Silverstein	1	90.00	90.00	90.00
	03/03/2019	Sales Receipt	1037	Allison Hoch	1	90.00	90.00	180.00
	03/03/2019	Sales Receipt	1036	Jim Dean	1	90.00	90.00	270.00
	03/04/2019	Sales Receipt	1039	Hugo Reyson	1	90.00	90.00	360.00
	03/08/2019	Sales Receipt	1050	Richard Halpert	1	90.00	90.00	450.00
	03/11/2019	Sales Receipt	1052	Jack Sheppert	1	90.00	90.00	540.00

MICHELLE L. LONG AND ANDREW S. LONG

	Date	Type	Num	Name	Qty	Sales Price	Amount	Balance
	03/19/2019	Sales Receipt	1058	Christian Sheppert	1	90.00	90.00	630.00
Total for Quarterly Membership					7		$ 630.00	
Registration Fee								
	03/03/2019	Sales Receipt	1038	Katie Layton	1	25.00	25.00	25.00
	03/10/2019	Sales Receipt	1051	John Lockhart	1	25.00	25.00	50.00
	03/13/2019	Sales Receipt	1053	Kate Austino	1	25.00	25.00	75.00
	03/18/2019	Sales Receipt	1057	Jim Sawyer	1	25.00	25.00	100.00
	03/21/2019	Sales Receipt	1060	Danielle Russell	1	25.00	25.00	125.00
	03/24/2019	Sales Receipt	1062	Benny Linus	1	25.00	25.00	150.00
Total for Registration Fee					6		$ 150.00	
Sports Drink								
Blue								
	03/07/2019	Sales Receipt	1049	Weekly Sales	2	2.00	4.00	4.00
	03/14/2019	Sales Receipt	1054	Weekly Sales	1	2.00	2.00	6.00
	03/21/2019	Sales Receipt	1061	Weekly Sales	3	2.00	6.00	12.00
	03/31/2019	Sales Receipt	1073	Weekly Sales	5	2.00	10.00	22.00
Total for Blue					11		$ 22.00	
Lemon								
	03/14/2019	Sales Receipt	1054	Weekly Sales	2	2.00	4.00	4.00
	03/31/2019	Sales Receipt	1073	Weekly Sales	3	2.00	6.00	10.00
Total for Lemon					5		$ 10.00	
Orange								
	03/07/2019	Sales Receipt	1049	Weekly Sales	4	2.00	8.00	8.00
	03/21/2019	Sales Receipt	1061	Weekly Sales	2	2.00	4.00	12.00
	03/31/2019	Sales Receipt	1073	Weekly Sales	3	2.00	6.00	18.00
Total for Orange					9		$ 18.00	
Red								
	03/07/2019	Sales Receipt	1049	Weekly Sales	3	2.00	6.00	6.00
	03/14/2019	Sales Receipt	1054	Weekly Sales	2	2.00	4.00	10.00
	03/21/2019	Sales Receipt	1061	Weekly Sales	1	2.00	2.00	12.00
Total for Red					6		$ 12.00	
Total for Sports Drink					31		$ 62.00	
Wicked Weights								
	03/07/2019	Sales Receipt	1043	Tim Barnes	1	50.00	50.00	50.00
	03/07/2019	Sales Receipt	1042	John Brown	1	50.00	50.00	100.00
Total for Wicked Weights					2		$ 100.00	
Yoga Fitness								
	03/07/2019	Sales Receipt	1047	Cindy Blackburn	1	50.00	50.00	50.00
	03/07/2019	Sales Receipt	1048	Jules Silverstein	1	50.00	50.00	100.00
Total for Yoga Fitness					2		$ 100.00	
TOTAL					138		$2,167.50	

Inventory Valuation Summary

Fitness Haven, LLC
Inventory Valuation Summary
As of March 31, 2019

	SKU	Qty	Asset Value	Calc. Avg
Bottled Water		53.00	9.01	0.17
Energy Drink				
Regular		40.00	42.00	1.05
Sugar-Free		6.00	6.30	1.05
Total Energy Drink			$ 48.30	
Nutrition Bar				
Chocolate		30.00	13.50	0.45
Peanut Butter		19.00	8.55	0.45
Vanilla		15.00	6.75	0.45
Total Nutrition Bar			$ 28.80	
Sports Drink				
Blue		53.00	19.61	0.37
Lemon		24.00	8.88	0.37
Orange		34.00	12.58	0.37
Red		14.00	5.18	0.37
Sugar-Free		0.00	0.00	
Total Sports Drink			$ 46.25	
TOTAL			$ 132.36	

Transaction List by Date (March)

Fitness Haven, LLC
Transaction List by Date
March 2019

Date	Transaction Type	Num	Name	Account	Split	Amount
03/01/2019	Check	1023	Great American Bank	Fitness Haven Checking	Visa	-68.97
03/01/2019	Sales Receipt	1034	Jules Silverstein	Undeposited Funds	Gym Revenues	90.00
03/01/2019	Sales Receipt	1035	Lynn Sampson	Undeposited Funds	Gym Revenues	35.00
03/02/2019	Bill		Cool T Shirts Co.	Accounts Payable (A/P)	Uniforms	45.00
03/03/2019	Sales Receipt	1036	Jim Dean	Undeposited Funds	-Split-	125.00
03/03/2019	Sales Receipt	1037	Allison Hoch	Undeposited Funds	Gym Revenues	90.00
03/03/2019	Sales Receipt	1038	Katie Layton	Undeposited Funds	-Split-	60.00
03/04/2019	Payment		Lucy Steele	Undeposited Funds	Accounts Receivable (A/R)	35.00
03/04/2019	Inventory Qty Adjust	14		Inventory Shrinkage	Inventory Asset	
03/04/2019	Sales Receipt	1039	Hugo Reyson	Undeposited Funds	Gym Revenues	90.00
03/06/2019	Check	1024	Copper Property Management Co.	Fitness Haven Checking	Rent & Lease	-1,500.00
03/07/2019	Sales Receipt	1040	Allison Hoch	Undeposited Funds	Gym Revenues	50.00
03/07/2019	Sales Receipt	1041	Jim Dean	Undeposited Funds	Gym Revenues	50.00
03/07/2019	Sales Receipt	1042	John Brown	Undeposited Funds	Gym Revenues	50.00
03/07/2019	Sales Receipt	1043	Tim Barnes	Undeposited Funds	Gym Revenues	50.00
03/07/2019	Sales Receipt	1044	Jerry Kline	Undeposited Funds	Gym Revenues	50.00
03/07/2019	Sales Receipt	1045	Adrian Gonzalez	Undeposited Funds	Gym Revenues	50.00
03/07/2019	Sales Receipt	1046	Lucy Steele	Undeposited Funds	Gym Revenues	50.00
03/07/2019	Sales Receipt	1047	Cindy Blackburn	Undeposited Funds	Gym Revenues	50.00
03/07/2019	Sales Receipt	1048	Jules Silverstein	Undeposited Funds	Gym Revenues	50.00
03/07/2019	Sales Receipt	1049	Weekly Sales	Undeposited Funds	-Split-	73.63
03/07/2019	Deposit			Fitness Haven Checking	-Split-	1,048.63
03/08/2019	Sales Receipt	1050	Richard Halpert	Undeposited Funds	Gym Revenues	90.00
03/09/2019	Check	1025		Fitness Haven Checking	Janitorial Expense	-250.00
03/10/2019	Sales Receipt	1051	John Lockhart	Undeposited Funds	-Split-	60.00
03/10/2019	Payment		Robert Markum	Undeposited Funds	Accounts Receivable (A/R)	35.00
03/11/2019	Bill Payment (Check)	1026	Cool T Shirts Co.	Fitness Haven Checking	Accounts Payable (A/P)	-45.00
03/11/2019	Purchase Order	1002	Fit Foods, Inc.	Accounts Payable (A/P)	-Split-	91.86
03/11/2019	Sales Receipt	1052	Jack Sheppert	Undeposited Funds	Gym Revenues	90.00
03/12/2019	Payment		Daniel Brown	Undeposited Funds	Accounts Receivable (A/R)	35.00
03/12/2019	Payment		Adrian Gonzalez	Undeposited Funds	Accounts Receivable (A/R)	35.00

03/13/2019	Sales Receipt	1053	Kate Austino	Undeposited Funds	-Split-	60.00
03/14/2019	Sales Receipt	1054	Weekly Sales	Undeposited Funds	-Split-	30.18
03/14/2019	Deposit			Fitness Haven Checking	-Split-	435.18
03/16/2019	Payment		Cindy Blackburn	Undeposited Funds	Accounts Receivable (A/R)	35.00
03/17/2019	Sales Receipt	1055	Cindy Blackburn	Undeposited Funds	Gym Revenues	35.00
03/17/2019	Sales Receipt	1056	Jim Dean	Undeposited Funds	Gym Revenues	35.00
03/18/2019	Sales Receipt	1057	Jim Sawyer	Undeposited Funds	-Split-	60.00
03/19/2019	Sales Receipt	1058	Christian Sheppert	Undeposited Funds	Gym Revenues	90.00
03/20/2019	Sales Receipt	1059	Kate Austino	Undeposited Funds	Gym Revenues	35.00
03/20/2019	Payment		Jerry Kline	Undeposited Funds	Accounts Receivable (A/R)	35.00
03/20/2019	Payment		Tim Barnes	Undeposited Funds	Accounts Receivable (A/R)	35.00
03/21/2019	Sales Receipt	1060	Danielle Russell	Undeposited Funds	-Split-	60.00
03/21/2019	Sales Receipt	1061	Weekly Sales	Undeposited Funds	-Split-	53.24
03/21/2019	Deposit			Fitness Haven Checking	-Split-	473.24
03/22/2019	Bill		Fit Foods, Inc.	Accounts Payable (A/P)	-Split-	84.24
03/24/2019	Sales Receipt	1062	Benny Linus	Undeposited Funds	-Split-	60.00
03/25/2019	Refund	1063	Benny Linus	Fitness Haven Checking	Gym Revenues	-35.00
03/26/2019	Invoice	1064	Adrian Gonzalez	Accounts Receivable (A/R)	Gym Revenues	35.00
03/26/2019	Invoice	1065	Lucy Steele	Accounts Receivable (A/R)	Gym Revenues	35.00
03/26/2019	Invoice	1066	Tim Barnes	Accounts Receivable (A/R)	Gym Revenues	35.00
03/26/2019	Invoice	1067	Robert Markum	Accounts Receivable (A/R)	Gym Revenues	35.00
03/26/2019	Invoice	1068	Katie Layton	Accounts Receivable (A/R)	Gym Revenues	35.00
03/26/2019	Invoice	1069	John Lockhart	Accounts Receivable (A/R)	Gym Revenues	35.00
03/26/2019	Invoice	1070	Kate Austino	Accounts Receivable (A/R)	Gym Revenues	35.00
03/26/2019	Invoice	1071	Jim Sawyer	Accounts Receivable (A/R)	Gym Revenues	35.00
03/27/2019	Check	1028	Rob's Repairs	Fitness Haven Checking	Repairs & Maintenance	-220.00
03/28/2019	Sales Receipt	1072	Adrian Gonzalez	Undeposited Funds	Gym Revenues	70.00
03/30/2019	Bill Payment (Check)	1029	City of Springfield	Fitness Haven Checking	Accounts Payable (A/P)	-86.45
03/30/2019	Bill Payment (Check)	1030	Metro Electric Co.	Fitness Haven Checking	Accounts Payable (A/P)	-178.86
03/30/2019	Bill Payment (Check)	1031	Time Warner	Fitness Haven Checking	Accounts Payable (A/P)	-147.62
03/30/2019	Bill Payment (Check)	1032	Waste Management	Fitness Haven Checking	Accounts Payable (A/P)	-45.00
03/30/2019	Bill Payment (Check)	1033	Fit Foods, Inc.	Fitness Haven Checking	Accounts Payable (A/P)	-84.24
03/31/2019	Bill		Time Warner	Accounts Payable (A/P)	Utilities:Phone/Internet	147.62
03/31/2019	Bill		Metro Electric Co.	Accounts Payable (A/P)	Utilities:Electric	128.86

73

03/31/2019	Bill		City of Springfield	Accounts Payable (A/P)	Utilities:Water	79.45
03/31/2019	Bill		Waste Management	Accounts Payable (A/P)	Utilities:Trash	45.00
03/31/2019	Sales Receipt	1073	Weekly Sales	Undeposited Funds	-Split-	94.45
03/31/2019	Deposit			Fitness Haven Checking	-Split-	224.45

Made in the USA
Las Vegas, NV
08 January 2022

40823976R00050